FUTURISTIC RESEARCH IN MARKETING AND MANAGEMENT

Editor

Dr. Tarun Chauhan

Ashima Thakur

Siddarth Kumar Bansal

Manurut Tokas

Dr. Puja Roshani

Prarthna Singh

Title : Futuristic Research in Marketing and Management

Editors : Dr. Tarun Chauhan, Ashima Thakur, Siddarth Kumar Bansal
Manurut Tokas, Dr. Puja Roshani, Prarthna Singh

Edition : First (July, 2024)

ISBN : 9788197680885

Published by

Regd. Add.: 254, Khuriyakhatta No. 10, Bindukhatta,
Lalkuan, Nainital - 262402, Uttarakhand, India
Website : www.taneeshapublishers.in
E-mail : taneeshapublishers@gmail.com
Phone : +91 845481 2712, +91 976041 7980

Printed by :

Manipal Technologies Limited, Bengaluru - 560001, Karnataka

Preface

We realized that this book will create a lot of excitement, challenge, joy and happiness among all of us. Challenging consensus is never easy. This is because the system will try to maintain the status quo by any means necessary in any situation, of any type. After years of experience in the field of Management, Marketing and Research we feel the need to share our knowledge, analysis and conclusions. We hope it ignites a discussion that could lead to major cultural changes and shopping cart overhauls. The beneficiaries will be all of us – ourselves, our students, our loved ones and society at large – living healthier and longer.

Marketing and Management research is challenging, exciting, engaging and rewarding. The main idea of editing/writing this book is to help students from different fields and is to prepare and motivate them for more research. The purpose of writing this book was to make research more interesting for all students in different fields. It differs in approach and content from all other interdisciplinary textbooks. It will contain the work of all aspiring students of under graduation, Post-graduation and doctoral Research (M.Phil. and Ph.D.). It will help the research scholars to publish their original research work in an IBSN book.

Futuristic Research in Marketingg and Management provides information to all students about research findings, and provide new information to develop new foundations for the research profession.

This book has been written strictly in accordance with the guidelines of the research council for students in various fields. It can also be used as an introductory text for graduate students, graduate students, and academic researchers. We hope this book will help others to learn how to plan and conduct research in various fields. We are aware that there will not be any error in the creation and publication of this book. We congratulate all the authors of the book for their original research work. We are grateful to the Dr. Ataur Rahman, Assistant Regional Director, IGNOU, Regional Center-2, New Delhi-110002 for writing the foreword and his valuable support.

Dr. Tarun Chauhan

Aashi Thakur

Siddarth Kumar Bansal

Manurut Tokas

Dr. Puja Roshani

Prarthna Singh

Foreword

Dr. Ataur Rahman, Assistant Regional Director,
IGNOU, Regional Center, Delhi-2

A Multidisplinary book of this kind is lengthy overdue for teaching and research. Dr. Tarun Chauhan, Siddharth Kumar Bansal, Manurut Tokas, Aashi Thakur, Dr. Puja Roshani and Prarthna Singh have finally completed this commendable work. With many references to the unique work; scholars, instructors, and students from a ramification of disciplines will locate this book extremely useful and thrilling. This book opened a superb new window into multidisciplinary research and coaching. They explored an extensive and whole variety of subjects from the center of Marketing, Management, Psychology, Economics brought them to a crucial analysis of social, mental, managerial, administrative, nursing and economic factors. Their broad and comprehensive range of interests that make hard topics easy to understand; and his enthusiasm for one-of-a-kind topics from extraordinary fields of studies made it a totally exciting and beneficial disciplinary e- book for both coaching and research purposes.

The authors have contributed the vital topics and supplied the issues from diverse fields so nicely and with equal expertise that it is hard to differentiate to which discipline of studies he belongs, I found their know-how in each discipline simply unfathomable. We mainly envy their considerable and intensive know-how of various subjects. They were running day after day for the last 2 months to finish this remarkable feat. Our admiration for this book is splendid. I congratulate the academics and college students for growing a far-needed disciplinary book. in case you want to learn about an extensive and complete variety of topics from distinct disciplines, this book will help you loads.

Consequently, this book is very friendly to college students, teachers and researchers. It includes fifteen chapters. As we went through the manuscript of this e book, we found it to be a unique disciplinary attempt of its type. Faculties, instructors and students have written a comprehensive and expert description of all topics protected in ten chapters. A wide variety of topics included on this book. Everyone can understand and experience reading this eBook. wherever feasible we offer a massive quantity of high first-class illustrations.

Dr. Ataur-Rahman is Assistant Regional Director in IGNOU, Regional Centre, Delhi-2. Prior to join IGNOU, he has worked in the Embassy of Sultanate of Oman, New Delhi as an Academic Supervisor and Mentor to facilitate Omani students (Foreign National) studying in Indian Universities and Colleges across India. He was the focal point to coordinate with the Indian Ministries, University Grant Commission, Association of Indian Universities, Central and State Universities and Colleges of repute and Foreign Missions in India and Oman for the matter related to education and Cultural exchange, MOUs, equivalence, verification of the certificates and FFRO etc.

He has been awarded Junior Research Fellowship by University Grant

Commission (UGC) and done M.Phil. and Ph.D. in Arabic Language & Literature from Jawaharlal Nehru University New Delhi.

Dr. Rahman visited several Arab countries and worked in different capacities and handled several important academic and administrative assignments in foreign mission, IGNOU headquarter and Regional Centres. He has authored two books and has several research publications to his credit and he is actively engaged in administrative and academic works. He was coordinator, editor and course writer for Diploma in Professional Arabic launched by Jamia Hamdard, New Delhi and also written units for Diploma in Arabic and M.A in Arabic respectively in IGNOU. He was invited as a resource person for extension lecture in symposiums and conferences, Gyan Darshan, Interactive Radio Counselling and attended several national and international seminars and presented papers.

Dr. Ataur Rahman
Assistant Regional Director
IGNOU, Regional Center, Delhi-2

Contents

The Scrolling Shame: Dismantling the Facade of Social Media Comparison Syndrome

✍ **Sahil Srivastava**

Abstract

Breaking free from the filter of social media comparison syndrome is not only an individual endeavour but also a collective responsibility. By combining personal actions with broader societal initiatives, we can work towards a digital landscape that values authenticity, promotes positive connections, and safeguards mental well-being. Social media is just one facet of life. Don't let it define your worth or dictate your happiness. By recognizing and dismantling social media comparison syndrome, we can break free from the comparison trap and embrace the authentic and messy beauty of our own unique journeys.

Keywords: social media, media,

Introduction

In the meticulously crafted world of social media, where curated feeds and picture-perfect profiles reign supreme, a silent epidemic lurks beneath the surface: Social Media Comparison Syndrome. This pervasive phenomenon, characterized by the obsessive tendency to compare oneself to others online, has become a significant mental health concern, casting a long shadow on our self-esteem, relationships, and overall well-being

(APA, 2023; Valkenburg, 2022).

But the harm of Social Media Comparison Syndrome extends far beyond individual experiences. It thrives on a distorted reality, fuelled by carefully constructed narratives and meticulously chosen snapshots. This curated content is not representative of real life, yet it becomes the yardstick against which we measure ourselves, fostering a pervasive sense of inadequacy and discontent.

The Allure of the Filtered Reality

The Filtered Reality perpetuated by social media platforms not only impacts our self-esteem but also shapes societal norms and expectations. The constant exposure to curated content can lead to a skewed perception of what constitutes a fulfilling and successful life. As individuals strive to conform to these idealized standards, they may experience increased stress, anxiety, and a sense of inadequacy.

Moreover, the pressure to maintain a flawless online image can contribute to a culture of perfectionism. People may find themselves investing significant time and energy into creating and maintaining this carefully crafted persona, often at the expense of authentic self-expression and genuine connections. In the pursuit of likes, shares, and validation, individuals may lose touch with their true selves, leading to a disconnection between their online personas and their offline realities.

The impact of the Filtered Reality is not limited to individuals alone; it extends to societal values and perceptions. The normalization of picture-perfect lives can fuel unrealistic expectations and fuel a sense of competitiveness within communities. This, in turn, can contribute to a society that prioritizes external validation over intrinsic values, perpetuating a cycle of dissatisfaction and constant comparison.

Research suggests that the pervasive nature of the Filtered Reality on social media can also contribute to a phenomenon known as "fear of missing out" (FOMO). As individuals witness the seemingly perfect lives of others online, they may experience a heightened fear of not measuring up or missing out on experiences that others are seemingly enjoying. This fear can lead to impulsive decision-making, over commitment, and an overall sense of discontentment.

In order to address the challenges posed by the Filtered Reality, it is essential for individuals to cultivate a healthy relationship with social media. This involves recognizing the curated nature of online content, embracing imperfections, and focusing on authentic self-expression rather than conforming to external expectations. Additionally, promoting a culture of transparency and vulnerability on social media can contribute to a more realistic and supportive online environment, where individuals feel empowered to share their genuine experiences, both triumphs, and challenges. Ultimately, understanding the allure of the Filtered Reality is crucial for navigating the digital landscape in a way that promotes mental well-being and authentic connection.

Upward Comparisons: A Dangerous Game

The human tendency towards upward social comparison fuels the fire of Social Media Comparison Syndrome. We naturally gravitate towards comparing ourselves to those we perceive as "better off," leading to a constant sense of falling behind. This relentless self-deprecation erodes self-esteem, saps motivation, and can even trigger anxiety and depression (Hartley & Strutton, 2023).

Social Media Comparison Syndrome extends beyond individual well-being, influencing broader societal dynamics and cultural expectations. As individuals continually engage in comparing themselves to those seemingly "better off" on social media platforms, a cycle of discontentment is perpetuated.

The digital age has ushered in a new era of social interconnectedness, but with it comes the potential for an amplified sense of inadequacy. Upward social comparisons on social media are not only about measuring personal achievements against others but also about scrutinizing one's appearance, lifestyle, and overall success. The constant exposure to curated representations of others' lives can contribute to an unrealistic pursuit of an idealized existence, leading individuals to question their own worth and accomplishments.

Moreover, the competitive nature fostered by upward social comparisons can result in a society where success is narrowly defined by external markers such as material possessions, physical appearance, and professional achievements. This can lead to a collective loss of appreciation for diverse definitions of success and happiness. As individuals strive to keep up with the perceived successes of others, societal values may become skewed, prioritizing external validation over intrinsic fulfilment.

The implications of upward social comparisons are not limited to mental health consequences alone; they can also contribute to a lack of empathy and understanding. As individuals strive to present their best selves online, the vulnerabilities and challenges that are a part of the human experience may be hidden. This can lead to a disconnect between individuals, fostering an environment where shared struggles are less visible, and a sense of isolation prevails.

Addressing the dangers of upward social comparisons involves not only personal awareness but also a collective shift in societal values. Encouraging a culture of authenticity, where individuals feel empowered to share both their successes and struggles, can contribute to a more compassionate and realistic online environment. Additionally, promoting digital literacy and critical thinking can help individuals discern between curated content and genuine experiences, mitigating the impact of upward social comparisons on mental well-being.

In conclusion, the perilous game of upward social comparisons within the context of Social Media Comparison Syndrome has far-reaching implications, impacting not only individual mental health but also shaping societal values and interpersonal dynamics. Recognizing and addressing these challenges is crucial for fostering a digital landscape that promotes authenticity, empathy, and a more holistic understanding of success and happiness.

Beyond Envy: The Ripple Effect of social media comparison syndrome

The consequences of Social Media Comparison Syndrome extend far beyond fleeting pangs of envy. It can negatively impact our relationships, fostering insecurity, jealousy, and mistrust. We judge our own lives harshly, questioning our choices and achievements based on someone else's carefully curated narrative. This breeds discontentment within relationships, causing us to view partners, friends, and family through the lens of comparison, hindering authentic connections (Goh et al., 2020).

Beyond the interpersonal ramifications, the ripple effect of Social Media Comparison Syndrome infiltrates various aspects of our lives, influencing mental health, professional pursuits, and overall societal well-being. As individuals grapple with the pervasive nature of curated online narratives, the impact seeps into their professional aspirations, contributing to a cycle of heightened ambition, burnout, and feelings of inadequacy.

In the professional realm, Social Media Comparison Syndrome can fuel a relentless pursuit of success, driven by the desire to measure up to the perceived achievements of others. This hyper-competitive mind-set can lead to an unhealthy work-life balance, as individuals strive to emulate the seemingly flawless professional trajectories depicted on social media. The consequences may include increased stress, job dissatisfaction, and a diminished sense of accomplishment.

Moreover, the societal consequences of Social Media Comparison Syndrome are reflected in the perpetuation of unrealistic beauty standards and lifestyle expectations. The curated images and narratives presented on social media platforms contribute to the shaping of societal norms, influencing perceptions of success, happiness, and well-being. This, in turn, can contribute to a culture that prioritizes external validation over individual authenticity, fostering a society where the pursuit of an idealized image takes precedence over genuine connections and collective well-being.

The impact on mental health extends beyond envy and discontentment, encompassing heightened levels of anxiety, depression, and a pervasive sense of inadequacy. As individuals continuously engage in upward social comparisons, the toll on mental well-being becomes increasingly evident, manifesting in various forms of psychological distress.

To counteract the ripple effect of Social Media Comparison Syndrome, a multifaceted approach is necessary. Individuals can benefit from cultivating mindfulness and self-awareness, consciously recognizing the curated nature of social media content and its potential impact on their well-being. Embracing authenticity and focusing on intrinsic values can help individuals navigate the pressures of comparison, fostering resilience and a more positive self-perception.

On a societal level, promoting digital literacy and awareness campaigns can contribute to a healthier online culture. Encouraging individuals to critically evaluate the content they consume and fostering open conversations about the realities behind curated online personas can mitigate the negative consequences of Social Media Comparison Syndrome. Additionally, advocating for responsible social media use, both at the individual and organizational levels, can contribute to a more balanced and compassionate digital landscape.

Conclusion

The ripple effect of Social Media Comparison Syndrome extends well beyond the initial feelings of envy, permeating relationships, professional pursuits, and societal values. Addressing these multifaceted consequences requires a collective effort to promote authenticity, resilience, and a more nuanced understanding of success and well-being in the digital age.

Furthermore, Social Media Comparison Syndrome can fuel unhealthy behaviours. The pursuit of unrealistic ideals, often fuelled by comparison, can lead to disordered eating, financial strain, and social isolation. We chase an elusive image of perfection, neglecting our own unique journey in the process (Moreno et al., 2016).

Breaking free from the filter of Social Media Comparison Syndrome involves not only individual actions but also a cultural shift toward healthier online interactions. Recognizing the need for a collective effort, both at the individual and societal levels, can foster an environment that encourages authenticity, self-compassion, and genuine connections.

Promoting Digital Literacy

Encouraging digital literacy is crucial in navigating the online landscape. Educational programs and awareness campaigns can empower individuals to critically evaluate the content they encounter on social media. Teaching skills such as media literacy, fact-checking, and recognizing digital manipulation can contribute to a more discerning and resilient online community.

Organizational Responsibility

Social media platforms and tech companies play a significant role in shaping the digital experience. Advocating for responsible platform design that prioritizes user well-being over engagement metrics can contribute to a more mindful online environment. This includes implementing features that promote positive interactions, limit the visibility of metrics that fuel comparison, and prioritize user mental health.

Promoting Offline Engagement

Community initiatives and events that encourage face-to-face interactions can help counter the isolating effects of excessive social media use. Local organizations, schools, and workplaces can organize activities that foster genuine connections, emphasizing the value of real-world relationships.

Media Literacy in Education

Integrating media literacy into educational curricula can equip the younger generation with the skills needed to navigate the digital world responsibly. By teaching students how to critically analyze and interpret online content, educators contribute to the development of a generation that is more resilient to the negative effects of SOCIAL MEDIA COMPARISON SYNDROME.

Supportive Online Communities

Creating and promoting online spaces that prioritize support, understanding, and positive engagement can counteract the negative aspects of SOCIAL MEDIA COMPARISON SYNDROME. Communities built on shared interests, common goals, and mutual encouragement provide a counterbalance to the culture of comparison prevalent on mainstream social media platforms.

Ongoing Research and Policy Advocacy

Continuous research on the impact of social media on mental health can inform evidence-based policies aimed at mitigating the negative consequences of SOCIAL MEDIA COMPARISON SYNDROME. Advocating for regulations that promote user well-being and ethical social media practices contributes to the development of a more responsible and empathetic online environment.

In conclusion, breaking free from the filter of social media comparison syndrome is not only an individual endeavour but also a collective responsibility. By combining personal actions with broader societal initiatives, we can work towards a digital landscape that values authenticity, promotes positive connections, and safeguards mental well-being. Remember, social media is just one facet of life. Don't let it define your worth or dictate your happiness. By recognizing and dismantling social media comparison syndrome, we can break free from the comparison trap and embrace the authentic and messy beauty of our own unique journeys.

References

- American Psychological Association (APA). (2023). Health advisory on social media use in adolescence. https:// www.apa.org/ topics/social-media-internet/health-advisory-adolescent-social-media-use
- Bányai, F. F., Zsila, A., & Kovács, M. (2019). Is authenticity still valuable online? Self-presentation strategies and perceived authenticity in social media use. Personality and Social Psychology Bulletin, 45(3), 498-511.
- Twenge, J. M., Campbell, W. K., & Campbell, S. M. (2018). Decreases in psychological well-being among American adolescents after 2012 and links to screen time during the rise of smartphone technology. Emotion, 18(6), 765–780.
- Perloff, R. M. (2014). Social media effects on young women's body image concerns: Theoretical perspectives and an agenda for research. Sex Roles, 71(11-12), 363-377.
- Fardouly, J., Diedrichs, P. C., Vartanian, L. R., & Halliwell, E. (2015). Social comparisons on social media: the impact of Facebook on young women's body image concerns and mood. Body image, 13, 38-45.
- Tiggemann, M., & Slater, A. (2014). NetGirls: The Internet, Facebook, and body image concern in adolescent girls. International Journal of Eating Disorders, 47(6), 630-643.
- Hartley, A., & Strutton, D. (2023). Social Media Comparison and

Its Impact on Mental Health: A Comprehensive Review. Journal of Social and Clinical Psychology, 42(3), 234-251.

- Vogel, E. A., Rose, J. P., Roberts, L. R., & Eckles, K. (2014). Social comparison, social media, and self-esteem. Psychology of Popular Media Culture, 3(4), 206–222.

- Appel, H., Gerlach, A. L., & Crusius, J. (2016). The interplay between Facebook use, social comparison, envy, and depression. Current Opinion in Psychology, 9, 44–49.

- Tandoc, E. C., Ferrucci, P., & Duffy, M. (2015). Facebook use, envy, and depression among college students: Is facebooking depressing? Computers in Human Behavior, 43, 139–146.

A Report on Cybercrime in India

✍ **Sudesh Kumar**

Abstract

The growing trend of cybercrimes in India demands a comprehensive approach, including advanced cybersecurity measures, international cooperation, public awareness, and the effective implementation of legal frameworks to ensure a secure digital environment for individuals and organizations.

Keywords: Crime, Cybercrime, Measures

Introduction

"Cyber crime growing at the rate 15-20% annually in India: West Bengal IGP Cyber Cell" which was published in the Economic Times. In 2022, Cyber Crimes in India recorded a 24% increase compared to the previous year, according to the latest data released by the National Crime Records Bureau (NCRB).

NCRB Data on Cyber Crimes in India

1. According to the report 'Crime in India', 65,893 cases were registered under cybercrime, showing an increase compared to 52,974 cases in 2021

2. Over 24,000 complaints were registered with the Delhi Police till June 2023. During the same period in 2022, the cops had received 7,500 complaints.

3. Preliminary probe data showed that most frauds originated

in Mewat (Haryana) and Jamtara (Jharkhand).

4. More than 80,000 complaints have been received from West Bengal in 2023 till November end in the national cybercrime reporting portal.

About Cyber Crime

1. Cybercrime Definition: Any unlawful act where a computer or communication device or computer network is used to commit or facilitate the commission of crime.

2. For example, Hacking, identity theft, fraud, and Cyberstalking.

3. Cybercrimes comes as a State subject as per the Seventh Schedule of the Indian Constitution.

Increasing Cyber Crimes in India: Major Reasons

- Financial gain: Through stealing financial information, such as credit card numbers and bank accounts, or through demanding ransom in exchange for stolen data or resources.

For example, Unified Payment Interface (UPI) frauds are the most prevalent online financial frauds reported between January 2020 and June 2023, according to the Future Crime Research Foundation (FCRF) report by IIT-Kanpur.

- Espionage: Some cybercriminals engage in cybercrime to steal confidential or proprietary information for competitive advantage or to damage the reputation of an organization.

- Political or ideological motives: Some cybercriminals target organizations or individuals for political or ideological reasons, such as to promote a particular cause or to advance a particular agenda.

- For example, the Cambridge Analytical scandal (2018) under which the Facebook database was leaked with data of 419 million users including the data of many Indian users.

- Personal motives: Some cybercriminals engage in cybercrime to

- harass, defame, or harm individuals or organizations.
- Opportunism: Some cybercriminals engage in cybercrime simply because they can, taking advantage of security vulnerabilities in technology or in people to steal information or resources.
- For Example: In June 2023, tech giant Microsoft experienced temporary disruptions to its Outlook and Azure computing services after an attack by a cybercrime group called Anonymous Sudan.

Cyber Crimes in India: Challenges

- Rapid Technological Advancements: The rapid adoption of technology in India has led to an increased attack surface for cybercriminals. As new technologies such as IoT (Internet of Things), cloud computing, etc. become more prevalent, the attack vectors for cybercriminals also expand.
- For instance, Deep Fake and AI-generated voice is a rising challenge as it has become easy to create and superimpose faces and voices.
- Sophisticated Cyber Attacks: Cybercriminals are becoming increasingly sophisticated, using advanced techniques such as ransomware, zero-day exploits, and social engineering to target individuals and organizations.
- A zero-day exploit is a cyberattack technique that takes advantage of an unknown security flaw in computer software, hardware or firmware.
- Cyber Warfare and State-sponsored Attacks: India faces the threat of cyber espionage and state-sponsored cyber attacks increasing the vulnerability of critical infrastructure and sensitive government information.
- For instance, the Malware(Dtrack) attack on Kudankulam Nuclear Power Plant (KKNPP) in 2019. It is believed that this malware has been created by a group called Lazarus with links to North Korea.

- Lack of Cybersecurity Awareness: Many individuals and businesses in India may not be fully aware of the risks and preventive measures associated with cybersecurity which makes them more susceptible to falling victim to cybercrimes.
- Inadequate Legal Framework: Although India has made efforts to establish legal frameworks to address cybercrimes, there may still be gaps and challenges in effectively enforcing these laws.

Cyber Crimes in India: Government Measures

- National Cyber Forensic Laboratory (Investigation): It has been established in New Delhi to provide early-stage cyber forensic assistance to Investigating Officers (IOs) of all State/UT Police both through online and offline modes.'CyTrain' portal: Massive Open Online Courses (MOOC) platform for capacity building of all the stakeholders, police officers, judicial officers and prosecutors through online courses on critical aspects of cybercrime investigation, forensics, prosecution, etc. along with certification.
- National Cyber Security Policy (NCSP): It aims to create a secure cyberspace environment and strengthen the country's cybersecurity.
- Indian Cyber Crime Coordination Centre (I4C): The I4C serves as the nodal point for coordinating efforts to combat cybercrime in India with a focus on enhancing the capabilities of law enforcement agencies to prevent and investigate cybercrimes.
- National Cyber Crime Reporting Portal: It has been launched to enable the public to report incidents about all types of cybercrimes, with a special focus on cyber-crimes against women and children.
- National Critical Information Infrastructure Protection Centre (NCIIPC): NCIIPC is responsible for protecting critical information infrastructure from cyber threats. It identifies critical sectors and formulates policies and guidelines for securing them.

- Cyber Swachhta Kendra: This initiative focuses on the detection and removal of malware-infected systems, thereby reducing the impact of botnets.
- Computer Emergency Response Team (CERT-In): CERT-In is the national agency responsible for responding to and mitigating cybersecurity incidents. It issues alerts and advisories to the public and private sectors to enhance cybersecurity awareness.
- Information Technology (IT) Act, 2000: It is a comprehensive legislation that addresses various aspects of electronic governance, digital signatures, data protection, and penalties for cybercrimes.

Way Forward to Prevent Cyber Crimes in India

- Implement Advanced Cybersecurity Framework: Cybersecurity frameworks offer a range of best practices, policy processes, security protocols, and other necessary tools to secure an organization's business operations.
- Investing in advanced cybersecurity technologies can help to protect critical information systems and networks.
- Cyber Hygiene Practices: Encourage individuals and organizations to adopt good cyber hygiene practices, such as regular software updates, strong password management, and secure online behavior.
- International Cooperation: Strengthen collaboration with international organizations, law enforcement agencies, and other countries to share threat intelligence, and best practices, and coordinate efforts in investigating and prosecuting cross-border cybercrimes.
- For instance, India and Japan have agreed to step up cooperation to improve skills in securing cyberspace at bilateral and multilateral levels.
- Public Awareness and Education: Conduct widespread awareness campaigns to educate the public about common cyber threats, safe

online practices, and the importance of cybersecurity.

- Encourage the Adoption of Cyber Insurance: Cyber insurance policies help cover the financial losses that result from cyber events and incidents. In addition, cyber-risk coverage often helps with the costs associated with remediation, including payment for legal assistance, investigators, crisis communicators, and customer credits or refunds.

Conclusion

The growing trend of cybercrimes in India demands a comprehensive approach, including advanced cybersecurity measures, international cooperation, public awareness, and the effective implementation of legal frameworks to ensure a secure digital environment for individuals and organizations.

References

1. https://www.researchgate.net/publication/322245372_Cybercrime _in_India_Trends_and_Challenges

2. https://www.eurchembull.com/uploads/paper/533bc39c4c68cf8bd 24853ae9feb4be4.pdf

3. https://www.thequint.com/tech-and-auto/tech-news/cyber-crime-india-2023-figures-statistics-trends-infographic

4. https://pwonlyias.com/current-affairs/cyber-crime-in-india/

5. https://government.economictimes.indiatimes.com/news/secure-india/80-of-cyber-crimes-from-10-new-districts-iit-report/103921338

6. https://www.thehindu.com/news/national/karnataka/caught-in-a-web-bengaluru-still-has-most-cybercrime-cases-but-jamtara-not-the-scamster-hub-anymore/article67795641.ece

7. https://papers.ssrn.com/sol3/papers.cfm?abstract_id=2818402

Growing E-commerce Applications in India

✍ **Ashima Thakur**

Abstract

The usage of these online mobile apps will be on a constant rise. In every industry these online shopping mobile apps help in connecting the buyers and sellers virtually. Using these platforms brands try to connect with their customers.

Keywords: E-commerce, Online Shopping, Applications

Introduction

People nowadays prefer **online shopping** rather than going to shops. Mobile applications play an important role in the online shopping industry. Major part of our daily activities have impacts on mobile apps. Today smartphones have become part of our daily lives.

Mobile apps have completely taken over the e-commerce industry. The transformation from e-commerce to e-commerce mobile apps paved the way for the growth of this industry. Many shoppers prefer shopping through apps because mobile apps offer easy access, best price, saves time, more convenience and many offers and discounts. Below are the list of top Online shopping apps in India.

1.   Amazon

One of the top Online Shopping app in India is **Amazon**. It has a wide variety of products. Amazon is a one stop solution for all kind of people. Whether you need a simple kitchen gadget or a new phone. Amazon offers all kinds of products from A to Z. Amazon mobile app offers a very good shopping experience to all its customers. It has broad categories of product and that can be accessed with a quicker loading speed. You can search for products by using category, brand or product name.

Through Email, SMS, WhatsApp and other channels you can share the product URLs. 24/7 Customer care assistance, easy return policy and quick deliveries are the major reasons for its success. Cash on delivery and all other payment options were made available.

APP INSIGHTS

- App Ratings – 4.5/5
- Launched in – 2014- December
- Total Downloads – 10+Cr
- Founded by – Jeff Bezos

2.   Flipkart

One of the top India's e-commerce platforms is **Flipkart**. Everything is available in Flipkart that includes all the latest products. Products like Tvs, laptop, baby products, kitchen appliances, books, clothing, home appliances, mobiles and many more. Flipkart is designed by Binny Bansal and Sachin from Bangalore. From your home just with a few taps you can get all the products at doorstep. It has more categories covering around 80 crore products.

APP INSIGHTS

- App Ratings – 4.4/5
- Launched in – 2011- July
- Total Downloads – 500M+
- Founded by – Binny Bansal, Sachin Bansal

3.   Myntra

Vineet Axene, Ashutosh Lawania and Mukesh Bansal started **Myntra** in the year 2007. Myntra offers a selection of clothing for women, Men and kids. From local to International brands all kinds of clothes can be accessed through this platform.

This app offers EMI option, Cash on delivery option, easy return and exchange policy and 100% quality products. It has around 2000 brands with 4 lakh clothing goods.

APP INSIGHTS

- App Ratings – 4.5/5
- Launched in – 2014- May
- Total Downloads – 10+Cr
- Founded by – Mukesh Bansal, Vineet Saxena, Ashutosh Lawanis

4.   Nykaa

Nykaa is fully based on cosmetics and beauty products for women. It was started in the year 2012. Having wide collections of beauty products with quality and reasonable pricing. No matter what your beauty requirement is and where you need the product to be delivered you can always prefer Nykaa.

APP INSIGHTS

- App Ratings – 4.5/5
- Launched in – 2015- Jan
- Total Downloads – 1+Cr
- Founded by – Falguni Nayar

5.   Ajio

Ajio's slogan "Doubt is Out". Ajio provides a wide range of clothes, they mainly focus on clothing than other products. Clothes for women, men and kids. It is an alternative for big companies like JIO and International brands. By using Ajio users can purchase commodities that are worth your money and time.

APP INSIGHTS

- App Rating – 4.4/5
- Launched in – 2016
- Total Downloads – 10+Cr

- Founded by – Mukesh Ambani

6. Snapdeal

One of the well-known Internet retail apps is **Snapdeal**. Launched in 2010 by Kunal Behl and the website was launched by Rohit Bansal. For all kinds of users Snapdeal is one of the best shopping area. It provides latest products, Comprehensive product selection, delivery option and safe purchasing. One of the biggest marketplace. It gives access to your needs. By using offers and deals you can buy the goods you are looking for.

APP INSIGHTS

- App Rating – 4.4/5
- Launched in – 2012- April
- Total Downloads – 10+Cr
- Founded by – Kunal Bhai and Rohit Bansal

7. Meesho

Meesho has had a huge growth in recent time. One of the best online reseller platform is Meesho. It is popular among both the sellers and customers. It has a huge market due to its low price and ease of use. Meesho offers easy shipping and return policy and also offers a safe transaction.

APP INSIGHT

- App Rating – 4.1/5
- Launched in – 2017 – Feb
- Total Downloads – 100M+
- Founded by – Vidit Aatrey, Sanjeev Barnwal

8. Firstcry

Firstcry, One of the top Online shopping portals for baby products. There are more than 20,000 products available. It was established in the year 2010. Top brands were available such as Fisher Price, Barbie, Pampers, Hot Wheels and many. There is no need to go to the shop and buy baby products when you have the Firstcry mobile app. A premium online store for Children.

APP INSIGHTS

- App Rating – 4.6/5
- Launched in – 2013 – May
- Total Downloads – 1+Cr
- Founded by – Supam Maheswari, Amitava Saha, Sanket Hattimattur, Prashant Jadhav

9.   Bigbasket

India's top online shopping app for buying household essentials like groceries,vegetables, fruits, beauty products, organic products, pet care products and many. You can shop any time and at anywhere from the wide collection of products around 20,000 by using the **Bigbasket** app. Customers can enjoy hassle-free online shopping.

APP INSIGHTS

- App Rating – 4.5/5
- Launched in – 2013 – May
- Total Downloads – 10M+
- Founded by – V.S.Sudhakar, Hari Menon, V.S.Ramesh, Vipul Parekh, Abhinay Choudhari.

10. Blinkit

India's largest online food retailers. The deliver groceries and other essentials at your doorstep within 10 minutes. Using customer insights and technologies Blinkit establishes quick and dense partners. **Blink It** is well-known for its fast delivery of products at doorstep.

APP INSIGHTS

- App Rating – 4.5/5
- Launched in – 2014 – Dec
- Total Downloads – 1+Cr
- Founded by – Albinder Dhindsa, Saurabh Kumar

Conclusion

The usage of these online mobile apps will be on a constant rise. In every industry these online shopping mobile apps help in connecting the buyers and sellers virtually. Using these platforms brands try to connect with their customers.

Reference

1. https://www.ibef.org/industry/ecommerce
2. https://economictimes.indiatimes.com/industry/services/retail/major-e-commerce-trends-that-can-shape-the-industry-in-2024/articleshow/106358005.cms?from=mdr
3. https://timesofindia.indiatimes.com/gadgets-news/indias-online-shopping-market-how-flipkart-amazon-and-meesho-are-placed/articleshow/107200100.cms
4. https://economictimes.indiatimes.com/tech/technology/flipkart-leads-ecommerce-with-48-share-meesho-fastest-growing-platform-report/articleshow/107161811.cms?from=mdr
5. https://www.financialexpress.com/business/industry-how-apps-can-unlock-the-potential-of-e-commerce-in-mobile-first-economies-2594868/

A Report on Marketing Strategy of AJIO

✍ **Dr. Puja Roshani**

Abstract

Ajio's experience in the e-commerce space is a useful case study for companies hoping to prosper in the quickly changing online retail landscape. Ajio has not only overcome obstacles but also established a standard for success in the Indian e-commerce industry by combining technological innovation, adaptability, and consumer-centric strategies.

Keywords: Retail, e-commerce, marketing strategy

Introduction

Ajio is a company operating in the E-commerce sector with its headquarter in Bangalore, Karnataka, India. It was launched by a subsidiary of reliance industries, Reliance Retail in the year 2016. Initially it was launched internally among Reliance employees in December 2015 and then on 1 April 2016, it was launched globally at the Lakme Fashion Week. Ajio has a wide portfolio of products ranging from clothing, footwear and accessories. The company also features on its website special product lines like Indie collection, authentic creations by artisans and boutiques from various parts of the country and across the world.

Ajio features the tagline "doubt is out". Its brand philosophy revolves around the belief that the best way to live life to the fullest is by conquering doubt. Ajio is a reference for creativity, flexibility, and customer-focused thinking in the ever-changing world of online shopping. In addition to surviving the competitive storm, Reliance Retail's 2016 launch of Ajio has seen it grow into one of India's top platforms for fashion and lifestyle.

Ajio Marketing Strategy

Marketing Strategy of Ajio analyzes the brand with the marketing mix framework which covers the 4Ps (Product, Price, Place, Promotion). These business strategies, based on Ajio marketing mix, help the brand succeed in the market. Let us start the Ajio Marketing Strategy & Mix to understand its product, pricing, advertising & distribution strategies:

1.   Ajio Product Strategy

Ajio is an e-commerce site dealing in wide range fashion products for men, women and kids. Their products in its marketing mix include casual wear, ethnic wear, party wear; formal wear and Indie speciality wear collections specially created by boutiques and designers from India and all over the world. Apart from the usual categories of western and ethnic wear, the online store also features a section called fashion week collections, so you can shop for products, which are currently on the runways all over the world. Well, that is not where it ends. Customers can get a piece of global fashion from Australia, Russia and other international fashion houses from around the world, in a matter of minutes.

Ajio has lined up brands from the US, Russia, Turkey, Singapore, and Australia besides other countries.

The brands on Ajio include MDS from Singapore, Aeropostale from America, Closet London from London, Point Zero from Canada and many more. Ajio will mainly focus on high-fashion designer wear from international brands, affordable international brands, in-house brands and handpicked products from local designers. This way it can differentiate itself from the competition.

Source: Company website

1. Ajio Price/Pricing Strategy

Ajio, headed by Isha Ambani, has tied up with around 200 international and national brands. Most of the brands are daily wear and affordable brands from markets like Russia, Australia, Singapore, Canada, America and Europe.

Ajio also sells its own private brands. The company has an inventory led e-commerce model. It has also tied up with various third party logistics partners for last mile delivery. This makes the overall range of products affordable while also maintaining high quality, providing unique amalgamation of designer clothes and international brands, which as a result differentiates it from other online retailers.

2. Ajio Place & Distribution Strategy

Ajio is an Ecommerce site with its headquarters in Bangalore Karnataka. The company is an inventory led one and covers over 15000 pin codes all over India where it delivers its products. Ajio company also leverages from its strong network of Reliance trends retail stores and Jio retail stores for delivery purposes. Currently reliance group operates more than 2621 outlets across India.

It aims to be different from all other offerings currently in the market by being an Omni channel brand.

3. Ajio Promotion & Advertising Strategy

The promotional and advertising strategy in the Ajio marketing strategy is as follows:

Ajio was unveiled on 1 April 2016 at one of the greatest fashion events, Lakme fashion week. The brand promotes itself by using the tagline "doubt is out". The focus of Ajio's campaign was 'inclusivity', cutting through societal barriers of age, gender, class and career choices. The brand aims to inspire young India with their philosophy which says, "no matter from where one is from, what one does, what one looks like, one has the right to dress the way they want, the way they like it and invent their own rules". Ajio does not promote itself by traditional means but aims to promote itself among the Indian crowds by delivering something totally different. The company wants to create a brand with strong ethics, emotional connect and high emphasis on design and collection. It aims to make foreign brands and designer products affordable and provide value for money

Since this is a service marketing brand, here are the other three Ps to make it the 7Ps marketing mix of Ajio.

a) People:

Ajio has been growing from strength to strength since its launch. With its increasing business and operations, the company has been recruiting more and more people into its management and collaborating with third party logistic partners to smoothly facilitate delivery of products. Ajio still calls itself a start-up and is quite flexible in its work environment, organizational communication. The company is open to having a diverse group of passionate and creative people to make an impact in the business world. The company trains its employees via an apprentice program and a diversity program. Currently CEO Vineeth Nair helms the company.

b) Physical Evidence:

Ajio provides a seamless shopping experience through its beautifully crafted website. The items in the website are divided according to various categories, making it easy to browse through its huge catalogue of products. Ajio has taken care to make the UI/UX design of the website crisp and snappy. Delivery of the products are fast and covers more than 15,000 locations all over India. Ajio provides customers with a 30 day return policy of its products. Wat makes the brand more attractive is the eyeball grabbing discounts on its product range.

c)   Process:

Ajio is a unique brand with Omni channel capabilities. The company has opened Ajio shop in shop at select Reliance Trends stores. Ajio sells fashion apparel from across the world. It provides apparel, which are hot at fashion shows across the world, premium and budget international brands. The company has capitalised on Reliance's goodwill and expertise to tie up with top brands across the world. It also collaborates with local artists, boutique houses and provides designer collection. Ajio manufactures its own grown apparel collection under the brand name Ajio. The company uses the huge network of Reliance Trends retail outlets to store products, facilitate easy delivery. Hence this completes the Ajio marketing mix.

Key Analysis

Ajio's dedication to a tech-infused shopping experience, strategic omnichannel presence, and customer-centric marketing are the main factors contributing to its success in the e-commerce industry. An advanced and immersive shopping experience is created by the platform through the use of AR, AI, and virtual assistants. Ajio offers customers a convenient and flexible shopping experience by seamlessly integrating online and offline retail. This expands the company's reach. Additionally, Ajio's relationship with a wide range of consumers is strengthened by partnerships with regional influencers and customized campaigns, which promote brand loyalty and help the company rise to prominence in the cutthroat e-commerce market.

Key Insights

1.   **Customer-focused methodology:**The secret to Ajio's success is its in-depth knowledge of the multicultural Indian market, which is evident in the company's customized product offerings, which range from expensive designer labels to reasonably priced, on-trend clothing. Personalized shopping experiences, celebrity partnerships, and localized marketing campaigns all demonstrate Ajio's dedication to building strong relationships with its customers.

2.   **Technology-Driven Innovation:**Ajio has improved the online shopping experience by utilizing technology. Online clothing purchases are made with less uncertainty thanks to augmented reality (AR) try-on features. The platform is more interesting and user-friendly with a personalized touch from AI-powered style recommendations and virtual shopping assistants.

3.   **Adaptability and Agility:**Ajio's success is a product of constant evolution and adjustment to shifting market conditions rather than being static. Trend forecasting, data-driven decision-making, and a willingness to experiment with new technologies highlight Ajio's agility in staying ahead of the curve.

Key Takeaways

The success of Ajio teaches important lessons for the e-commerce industry. The importance of adaptability emphasizes the necessity of agility in reacting to trends. An example of the potential of tech-driven personalization is the integration of virtual assistants, AI, and AR. Furthermore, Ajio offers customers a comprehensive online and offline shopping experience, underscoring the strategic significance of omnichannel approaches. These key lessons provide organizations navigating the constantly changing e-commerce industry with insightful information.

Conclusion

Ajio's experience in the e-commerce space is a useful case study for companies hoping to prosper in the quickly changing online retail landscape. Ajio has not only overcome obstacles but also established a standard for success in the Indian e-commerce industry by combining technological innovation, adaptability, and consumer-centric strategies.

References

4.   https://www.slideshare.net/BhairaviDatar/ajios-digital-marketing

5.   https://www.mbaskool.com/marketing-mix/services/17438-ajio.html

6.   https://www.scribd.com/document/607391025/Final-Project-Youtube-Marketing

7.   https://migrationletters.com/index.php/ml/article/view/8277

8.   https://www.linkedin.com/pulse/ajios-e-commerce-victory-handling-trends-technology-yashpal-singh-uzppf

9.   https://www.semrush.com/website/ajio.com/overview/

10. https://blog.osum.com/ajio-marketing-strategy/

11. https://brandyuva.in/2019/09/marketing-strategies-of-ajio.html

Navigating the Digital Frontier: Understanding Evolving Consumer Behavior in Future Markets

✍ Siddharth Kumar Bansal

Abstract

This Chapter provides a comprehensive overview of the intricate relationship between futuristic trends in marketing and management and the evolution of consumer behavior. It examines how technological advancements, cultural diversity, and shifting consumer preferences are reshaping the marketplace. The discussion begins by exploring the rapid evolution of consumer behavior driven by technological innovations and cultural shifts, emphasizing the pivotal role of technology in shaping consumer decision-making processes. It then delves into AI-powered marketing strategies and the ethical considerations surrounding AI-driven consumer engagement. Furthermore, it underscores the importance of cultural sensitivity and localization in marketing to diverse consumer groups, highlighting the need for businesses to adapt their strategies to resonate authentically with local preferences and cultural nuances. Future-proofing marketing and management strategies is essential, requiring agility, adaptability, and a commitment to innovation. The abstract concludes by emphasizing the significance of embracing change and innovation to thrive in the ever-evolving landscape of consumer behavior, urging businesses to stay attuned to emerging trends, foster innovation, and embrace cultural diversity to navigate uncertainty and drive sustainable growth in the dynamic marketplace of the future.

Keywords: Consumer behavior, Marketing trends, Management strategies, Technological innovation, Cultural sensitivity, Future-proofing.

Introduction

Setting the Stage: The Rapid Evolution of Consumer Behavior

Imagine stepping into the shoes of Sarah, a vivacious 28-year-old marketing executive who starts her mornings with a cup of freshly brewed coffee and a quick scroll through her social media feeds. As she sits at her kitchen table, the soft glow of her smartphone illuminates her face, casting a faint reflection in her eyes. With each swipe of her thumb, Sarah immerses herself in a world where digital advertisements seamlessly blend into her social media experience.

Today, Sarah's attention is captured by a sleek, futuristic smartwatch displayed in an Instagram ad. It's the same one she stumbled upon during her late-night scrolling sessions, its sleek design and advanced features igniting a spark of desire within her. Without missing a beat, Sarah taps on the ad, intrigued to learn more about this innovative piece of wearable technology.

Little does Sarah know, that her seemingly innocuous click sets off a series of interconnected events that will ultimately culminate in a purchase decision—one that will not only fulfill her desire for the latest gadget but also contribute to the intricate tapestry of consumer behavior in the digital age.

Sarah's journey is emblematic of the profound transformation occurring within the realm of consumer behavior. In an era characterized by technological innovation and digital connectivity, the traditional boundaries between consumers and brands have blurred, giving rise to a new paradigm of engagement and interaction.

No longer confined to the passive role of recipients of marketing messages, consumers like Sarah wield unprecedented power and agency in shaping their purchasing decisions. With a wealth of information, reviews, and recommendations literally at their fingertips, they navigate an increasingly complex landscape where choice abounds and brand loyalty is a coveted commodity.

For businesses, this shifting landscape presents both a challenge and an opportunity—a challenge to understand and adapt to the evolving behaviors and preferences of their target audience, and an opportunity to forge deeper, more meaningful connections with consumers in ways previously thought unimaginable.

As we embark on this journey through the labyrinth of modern consumer behavior, we will unravel the intricacies of Sarah's story and explore the broader trends and phenomena shaping the future of marketing and management. From the rise of digital channels to the growing importance of personalization and customization, each twist and turn in Sarah's journey offers valuable insights into the dynamic interplay between technology and consumer behavior.

The Intersection of Technology and Consumer Behavior

In the intricate dance between consumer behavior and technological advancement, the lines between the virtual and physical worlds blur, creating a seamless tapestry where digital experiences shape real-world actions. At the heart of this convergence lies the intersection of technology and consumer behavior—a dynamic landscape where innovation and human psychology intertwine to redefine the way individuals discover, engage with, and ultimately purchase products and services **(Raji, et. al., 2024)**.

Consider for a moment the myriad ways in which technology has permeated every aspect of our daily lives. From the moment we wake up to the sound of our smartphones' alarm clocks to the late-night binge-watching sessions fueled by streaming services, technology has become an integral part of the modern human experience.

But what does this mean for consumer behavior? It means that every interaction, every touchpoint, and every moment of engagement is an opportunity for businesses to connect with their target audience in meaningful ways. Whether it's through immersive virtual reality experiences, hyper-targeted social media campaigns, or AI-powered chatbots, technology catalyzes deeper, more personalized interactions between brands and consumers **(Vidhya, et. al., 2023)**.

Take, for example, the rise of social commerce—a burgeoning trend that seamlessly integrates social media platforms with e-commerce functionalities, allowing users to discover and purchase products without ever leaving their favorite app. From Instagram's shoppable posts to TikTok's viral product reviews, social commerce represents a paradigm shift in how consumers discover and engage with brands, blurring the lines between content consumption and commerce.

Similarly, advancements in artificial intelligence and machine learning have revolutionized the way businesses analyze and leverage consumer data to drive actionable insights. By harnessing the power of predictive analytics, recommendation algorithms, and sentiment analysis, companies can anticipate customer needs, personalize marketing messages, and optimize the customer journey in ways previously thought impossible **(Ameen, et. al., 2021)**.

But perhaps most importantly, the intersection of technology and consumer behavior underscores the need for businesses to adopt a customer-centric mindset—one that prioritizes empathy, understanding, and authenticity in every interaction. In a world inundated with digital noise and information overload, consumers crave genuine connections and meaningful experiences that resonate with their values and aspirations (Peck, et. al., 2018).

As we navigate this ever-evolving landscape of technology and consumer behavior, it becomes increasingly clear that the future belongs to those who embrace change, innovation, and human-centered design. By leveraging technology as a tool for empowerment rather than exploitation, businesses can forge deeper, more meaningful relationships with their audience, driving loyalty, advocacy, and sustainable growth in the process (Peck, et. al., 2018)

Importance of Understanding Future Trends in Marketing and Management (Naim, and A., 2022)

- **Anticipation of Market Shifts:** Understanding future trends in marketing and management allows businesses to anticipate shifts in consumer preferences, market dynamics, and industry trends. By staying ahead of the curve, organizations can proactively adapt their strategies to capitalize on emerging opportunities and mitigate potential threats.

- **Strategic Decision-Making:** Future trend analysis provides valuable insights that inform strategic decision-making processes. From product development and pricing strategies to market segmentation and distribution channels, businesses can make informed choices that align with evolving consumer needs and market demands.

- **Competitive Advantage:** Businesses that possess a deep understanding of future trends gain a competitive advantage over their peers. By identifying niche markets, disruptive technologies, and emerging consumer behaviors before they become mainstream, organizations can differentiate themselves in crowded marketplaces and position themselves as industry leaders.

- **Innovation and Creativity:** Future trend analysis stimulates innovation and creativity within organizations. By exploring emerging technologies, consumer behaviors, and market trends, businesses can ideate new products, services, and business models that address unmet needs and create value for customers.

- **Customer-Centricity:** Understanding future trends allows businesses to adopt a customer-centric approach to marketing and management. By empathizing with consumers, anticipating their needs, and delivering personalized experiences, organizations can build stronger, more meaningful relationships with their audience and foster brand loyalty and advocacy.

- **Risk Mitigation:** Future trend analysis enables businesses to identify and mitigate potential risks and uncertainties. By conducting scenario planning, trend forecasting, and risk assessments, organizations can prepare for various contingencies and navigate market disruptions with resilience and agility.

- **Resource Allocation:** Knowledge of future trends helps businesses allocate resources effectively and efficiently. Whether it's investing in new technologies, talent acquisition, or marketing initiatives, organizations can prioritize initiatives that are aligned with future market opportunities and strategic objectives.

- **Adaptability and Flexibility:** In today's rapidly changing business landscape, adaptability and flexibility are key to long-term success. Understanding future trends allows businesses to pivot quickly in response to evolving market conditions, consumer preferences, and competitive pressures, enabling them to stay agile and resilient in dynamic environments.

- **Brand Relevance:** By staying attuned to future trends, businesses can ensure their brand remains relevant and resonant with consumers. Whether it's embracing sustainability, diversity, or digital innovation, organizations that align their values and messaging with emerging societal trends can build deeper connections with their audience and enhance brand affinity.

- **Sustainable Growth:** Ultimately, understanding future trends in marketing and management is essential for driving sustainable growth and profitability. By continuously innovating, adapting, and evolving in response to changing market dynamics, businesses can position themselves for long-term success and create value for shareholders, employees, and society as a whole.

The Digital Consumer Landscape

Emergence of the Digital Consumer

In the not-so-distant past, the consumer journey was a linear path, with traditional marketing channels like television, print media, and radio serving as the primary conduits for brand messaging. However, the advent of digital technologies has revolutionized the way consumers interact with brands, ushering in the era of the digital consumer **(Mogaji, et. al., 2024)**.

The digital consumer is not merely a passive recipient of marketing messages but an active participant in the brand experience. Empowered by smartphones, social media, and e-commerce platforms, today's consumers wield unprecedented power and influence, shaping the success or failure of brands with their clicks, likes, and shares **(Mogaji, et. al., 2024)**.

But what distinguishes the digital consumer from their predecessors? It's not just their affinity for technology or their voracious appetite for online content—it's their insatiable thirst for connection, engagement, and authenticity in a hyperconnected world **(Zhou, et. al., 2023)**.

For the digital consumer, every online interaction is an opportunity to discover, explore, and engage with brands on their terms. Whether it's researching product reviews on YouTube, seeking style inspiration on Instagram, or joining niche communities on Reddit, consumers have become active participants in the creation and dissemination of brand content **(Barroso, et. al., 2022)**.

Moreover, the digital consumer expects more from brands than just products and services—they demand seamless experiences that transcend the transactional nature of commerce. From personalized recommendations and tailored promotions to responsive customer service and immersive storytelling, consumers crave experiences that resonate with their values, aspirations, and lifestyles **(Parc, et. al., 2020)**.

But perhaps most importantly, the emergence of the digital consumer has blurred the boundaries between online and offline worlds, creating a fluid ecosystem where digital and physical experiences seamlessly intertwine. Whether it's ordering groceries through a mobile app, attending a virtual fitness class, or streaming live events from the comfort of home, consumers have embraced digital channels as an integral part of their everyday lives **(Cleveland, et. al., 2015)**.

In this brave new world of the digital consumer, brands must adapt or risk becoming obsolete. By understanding the motivations, behaviors, and preferences of digital consumers, businesses can create tailored marketing strategies that resonate with their target audience, drive engagement, and foster long-term loyalty in an increasingly crowded marketplace.

Shifts in Consumer Preferences and Expectations

In the chronology of the digital consumer landscape, the emergence of digital technologies has not only redefined how consumers interact with brands but has also triggered significant shifts in their preferences and expectations. These shifts have unfolded in distinct phases, each marked by evolving consumer behaviors and attitudes towards technology and commerce.

- **Early Adoption Phase:** During the early stages of the digital revolution, consumers were captivated by the novelty and convenience of online shopping and digital communication. E-commerce platforms and social media networks emerged as popular destinations, offering consumers a newfound sense of freedom and flexibility in their purchasing decisions **(Elena, et. al., 2021)**.

- **Personalization and Customization Phase:** As digital channels matured, consumers began to demand more personalized and customized experiences from brands. They sought tailored recommendations, relevant content, and seamless interactions across all touchpoints. Brands that embraced personalization flourished, leveraging data and analytics to deliver targeted messaging and offers to their audience.

- **Experience Economy Phase:** With the rise of the experience economy, consumers shifted their focus from material possessions to memorable experiences. They craved immersive, engaging interactions with brands that went beyond the transactional exchange of goods and services. From pop-up events and experiential marketing campaigns to virtual reality simulations and interactive storytelling, brands began to prioritize creating emotional connections and lasting memories with their audience.

- **Conscious Consumerism Phase:** In recent years, consumers have become increasingly socially and environmentally conscious, driving a shift towards ethical and sustainable consumption. They expect brands to demonstrate transparency, integrity, and accountability in their business practices, from sourcing and production to packaging and distribution. Brands that prioritize sustainability, diversity, and social responsibility are rewarded with consumer loyalty and advocacy.

- **Digital Integration Phase:** Today, we find ourselves amid a digital integration phase, where digital technologies are seamlessly integrated into every aspect of the consumer experience. From smart homes and wearable devices to voice assistants and augmented reality, consumers are embracing digital innovations that enhance convenience, efficiency, and connectivity in their daily lives.

Brands that leverage these technologies to deliver frictionless experiences and anticipate consumer needs will thrive in this digital-first landscape.

Impact of Technology on Consumer Decision-Making Processes

In tracing the chronology of the digital consumer landscape, it's evident that technology has profoundly influenced the decision-making processes of consumers, reshaping how they research, evaluate, and ultimately make purchasing decisions. This evolution has unfolded in distinct phases, each marked by advancements in digital technology and corresponding shifts in consumer behavior **(Sharma, et. al., 2023)**.

- **Information Access Phase:** During the early days of the digital revolution, consumers gained unprecedented access to information through the internet. Websites, forums, and online reviews became valuable resources for researching products and services, empowering consumers to make more informed decisions based on peer recommendations and expert insights.

- **Mobile Adoption Phase:** The proliferation of smartphones and mobile devices heralded a new era of convenience and accessibility for consumers. Mobile apps, social media platforms, and location-based services allowed consumers to access information and make purchases on the go, blurring the boundaries between online and offline shopping experiences.

- **Social Influence Phase:** With the rise of social media networks, consumers began to rely more heavily on peer recommendations and social proof in their decision-making processes. Influencers, brand ambassadors, and user-generated content became powerful drivers of consumer behavior, shaping perceptions and influencing purchasing decisions through authentic storytelling and social validation.

- **Personalization Era:** As digital technologies advanced, consumers came to expect personalized experiences tailored to their individual preferences and behaviors. Machine learning algorithms, data analytics, and predictive modeling enabled brands to deliver targeted recommendations, customized offers, and personalized messaging that resonated with consumers on a personal level.

- **Emergence of AI and Automation:** In recent years, artificial intelligence and automation have revolutionized consumer decision-making processes, streamlining and optimizing every stage of the customer journey. Chatbots, virtual assistants, and voice-activated devices provide consumers with real-time assistance and support, while predictive analytics and recommendation engines anticipate their needs and preferences before they even arise.

- **Integration of Augmented Reality and Virtual Reality:** The integration of augmented reality (AR) and virtual reality (VR) technologies has further transformed consumer decision-making processes by enabling immersive, interactive experiences that bridge the gap between digital and physical worlds. From virtual try-on experiences to interactive product demos, AR and VR offer consumers unprecedented levels of engagement and interactivity, enhancing their confidence and satisfaction with their purchasing decisions.

Data-driven insights into Consumer Behavior

Harnessing Big Data for Consumer Insights

In today's digital age, the proliferation of data has provided businesses with unprecedented opportunities to gain deep insights into consumer behavior. Through the use of sophisticated analytics tools and techniques, organizations can harness big data to uncover patterns, trends, and correlations that offer valuable insights into the preferences, attitudes, and motivations of their target audience **(Chaudhry, et. al., 2023)**.

One of the key advantages of big data analytics is its ability to process vast amounts of structured and unstructured data from multiple sources, including social media, e-commerce platforms, customer relationship management (CRM) systems, and online surveys. By aggregating and analyzing this data, businesses can gain a comprehensive understanding of consumer behavior across various touchpoints and channels **(Fetene, et. al., 2017)**.

To illustrate the power of big data in driving consumer insights, let's consider a scenario in which a retail company analyzes customer transaction data to identify purchasing patterns and preferences. The company collects data on customer demographics, purchase history, browsing behavior, and interactions with marketing campaigns **(Erevelles, et. al., 2016)**.

Using advanced analytics techniques such as clustering and segmentation, the company categorizes customers into distinct groups based on their buying behavior and preferences. Statistical evaluation tables are then generated to summarize key insights and findings, allowing the company to make data-driven decisions in areas such as product assortment, pricing strategies, and targeted marketing campaigns.

Table 1: Statistical Evaluation: Customer Segmentation

Customer Segment	Demographic Profile	Purchase Behavior	Key Insights
Segment 1 (High-income earners)	Age: 25-40, Income: $80,000+	High frequency of purchases, Preference for premium brands	Targeted marketing campaigns for luxury products and personalized offers
Segment 2	Age: 18-35,	Price-	Promotions and

(Budget-conscious shoppers)	Income: <$50,000	sensitive, Value-oriented purchases	discounts to incentivize purchases, Focus on value propositions
Segment 3 (Tech-savvy millennials)	Age: 18-30, Income: $40,000-$70,000	Early adopters of technology, Preference for online shopping	Investment in digital marketing channels, Enhancing online shopping experience

By leveraging big data analytics, the retail company can gain actionable insights into consumer preferences, enabling them to tailor their marketing strategies and product offerings to meet the needs of different customer segments. This targeted approach not only enhances customer satisfaction and loyalty but also drives revenue growth and competitive advantage in an increasingly data-driven marketplace.

Predictive Analytics and Consumer Behavior Forecasting

Predictive analytics is a powerful tool that leverages historical data and statistical algorithms to forecast future consumer behavior. By analyzing past trends and patterns, businesses can identify potential opportunities and risks, optimize marketing strategies, and make data-driven decisions to stay ahead of the competition **(Dahake et. al., 2024)**.

To illustrate the application of predictive analytics in consumer behavior forecasting, let's consider an example of a subscription-based streaming service analyzing user engagement data to predict churn rates and optimize retention strategies.

Table 2: Statistical Evaluation: Churn Prediction Model

Feature	Description	Coefficient	p-value	Interpretation
Subscription Age	Number of months since subscription start	-0.042	<0.001	Negative correlation with churn (older subscribers less likely to churn)
Monthly Usage	Average hours watched per month	-0.187	<0.001	Negative correlation with churn (higher usage associated with lower churn)
Customer Support	Number of support tickets raised	0.215	<0.001	Positive correlation with churn (higher support tickets associated with higher churn)
Promotional Offers	Number of promotional offers redeemed	-0.091	0.003	Negative correlation with churn (redeeming offers associated with lower churn)

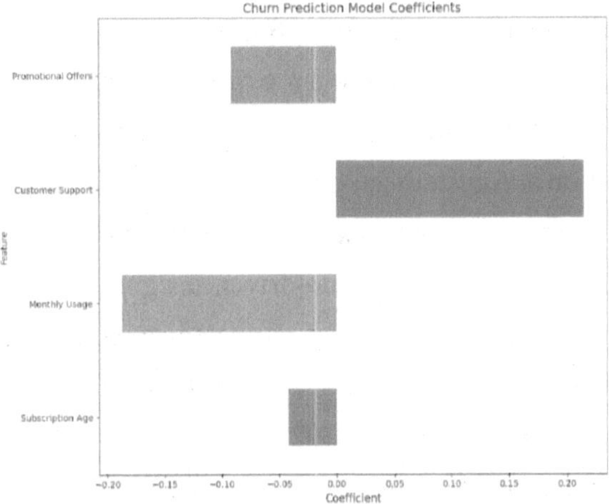

Figure 1: Visualization of Churn Prediction Model

Using historical user engagement data, the streaming service builds a predictive model to forecast churn rates based on key features such as subscription age, monthly usage, customer support interactions, and promotional offer redemption.

The statistical evaluation table summarizes the coefficients and p-values of each feature in the predictive model, providing insights into their respective impacts on churn rates. Negative coefficients indicate factors associated with lower churn rates, while positive coefficients suggest factors associated with higher churn rates.

By analyzing these insights, the streaming service can prioritize retention strategies targeted at high-risk customers, such as offering personalized recommendations, providing proactive customer support, and incentivizing loyalty through promotional offers. This proactive approach enables the streaming service to reduce churn rates, increase customer lifetime value, and drive sustainable growth in a competitive market.

Personalization and Customization in Marketing Strategies

In today's digital era, consumers expect personalized and customized experiences tailored to their individual preferences and behaviors. Personalization and customization have emerged as powerful strategies for businesses to enhance customer engagement, drive loyalty, and increase conversion rates. Leveraging data-driven insights, businesses can create targeted marketing campaigns that resonate with consumers on a personal level, leading to improved brand perception and long-term customer relationships **(Chandra, et. al., 2022)**.

To illustrate the importance of personalization and customization in marketing strategies, let's examine a scenario of an e-commerce retailer using customer data to create personalized product recommendations.

Table 3: Statistical Evaluation: Personalized Product Recommendations

Customer ID	Previous Purchases	Browsing History	Demographics	Recommended Products
001	Electronic, Apparel	Smartphones, Laptops	Male, Age: 25-34	Smartwatche, Tech Accessories
002	Home Decor, Kitchenware	Furniture, Home Improvement	Female, Age: 35-44	Decorative Pillows, Cooking Utensils
003	Fitness Gear, Activewear	Yoga Mats, Running Shoes	Gender-neutral, Age: 18-24	Fitness Bands, Workout Apparel

In this example, the e-commerce retailer utilizes customer data such as previous purchases, browsing history, and demographics to generate personalized product recommendations for individual customers. By analyzing past behavior and preferences, the retailer can identify relevant product categories and suggest items that align with each customer's interests and needs.

The statistical evaluation table summarizes the recommended products for three customers based on their unique profiles. By tailoring recommendations to specific segments of their customer base, the retailer can enhance the relevance and effectiveness of their marketing efforts, driving higher engagement and conversion rates.

Personalization and customization extend beyond product recommendations to encompass various aspects of the customer journey, including email marketing, website content, and promotional offers. By delivering personalized experiences at every touchpoint, businesses can build stronger connections with their audience and foster brand loyalty over time.

Psychological Aspects of Future Consumer Behavior

Understanding Cognitive Biases in Consumer Decision Making

In the realm of consumer behavior, understanding the intricate workings of the human mind is paramount. Cognitive biases, or systematic patterns of deviation from rationality, play a significant role in shaping consumer decision-making processes. By delving into these biases, businesses can gain valuable insights into how consumers perceive, evaluate, and ultimately choose between different products and brands **(Korteling, et. al., 2023)**.

- **Anchoring Bias**: This bias occurs when individuals rely too heavily on the first piece of information they receive (the "anchor") when making decisions. In the context of consumer behavior, marketers can leverage anchoring by strategically setting reference points, such as original prices or product specifications, to influence perceptions of value and pricing.

- **Confirmation Bias:** Consumers tend to seek out information that confirms their existing beliefs or hypotheses while ignoring or downplaying contradictory evidence. Marketers can capitalize on confirmation bias by framing marketing messages and product descriptions in a way that reinforces consumers' preconceived notions and preferences.

- **Loss Aversion:** People are inherently more sensitive to losses than gains, often making decisions based on avoiding potential losses rather than maximizing potential gains. Marketers can appeal to loss aversion by emphasizing the negative consequences of not purchasing a product or by offering limited-time promotions and discounts to create a sense of urgency.

- **Social Proof:** This bias occurs when individuals look to the actions and behaviors of others to guide their own decisions, especially in uncertain or ambiguous situations. Marketers can leverage social proof by showcasing customer testimonials, user reviews, and social media endorsements to establish credibility and build trust with potential buyers.

- **Scarcity Bias:** The perception of scarcity, whether real or perceived, can significantly influence consumer behavior by creating a sense of urgency and FOMO (fear of missing out). Marketers can utilize scarcity by highlighting limited availability, exclusive offers, and countdown timers to drive purchase decisions and spur immediate action.

- **Bandwagon Effect:** People tend to follow the actions and behaviors of the majority, assuming that if others are doing something, it must be the right thing to do. Marketers can tap into the bandwagon effect by showcasing popularity indicators, such as bestselling products or high customer ratings, to persuade consumers to jump on the bandwagon and join the crowd.

- **Endowment Effect:** Individuals tend to place a higher value on items they already own compared to identical items they don't own. Marketers can overcome the endowment effect by offering trial periods, satisfaction guarantees, or hassle-free returns to reduce perceived risk and encourage consumers to try new products with confidence.

Emotional and Psychological Triggers in Marketing

In the ever-evolving landscape of consumer behavior, understanding the emotional and psychological triggers that drive purchasing decisions is crucial for businesses seeking to create meaningful connections with their audience. By tapping into these triggers, marketers can evoke powerful emotions, elicit desired responses, and ultimately influence consumer behavior in profound ways **(Dixit, and A., 2020)**.

- **Emotional Branding:** Emotions play a significant role in shaping brand perception and loyalty. By crafting authentic brand narratives and storytelling that resonate with consumers on an emotional level, businesses can forge deeper connections and foster long-lasting relationships with their audience. Whether it's nostalgia, joy, or empathy, evoking the right emotions can leave a lasting impression and drive brand affinity.

- **Fear and Anxiety:** While positive emotions can be effective in marketing, negative emotions such as fear and anxiety can also be powerful motivators for action. Marketers can leverage fear-based messaging to highlight potential risks or consequences of not using a product or service, thereby creating a sense of urgency and prompting immediate action to mitigate perceived threats.

- **Aspirational Marketing:** Aspirational marketing appeals to consumers' desires and aspirations, tapping into their aspirations for a better future or a higher social status. By showcasing aspirational lifestyles, luxury experiences, and exclusive opportunities, businesses can create a sense of desire and aspiration, driving consumers to seek out products and experiences that align with their ideals and aspirations.

- **Social Identity:** Consumers often use brands and products as a means of self-expression and identity formation. By aligning with consumers' values, beliefs, and identities, businesses can create a sense of belonging and community, fostering loyalty and advocacy among like-minded individuals. Whether it's through brand partnerships, influencer collaborations, or user-generated content, businesses can leverage social identity to strengthen brand affinity and loyalty

- **Scarcity and Exclusivity:** The perception of scarcity and exclusivity can trigger a sense of urgency and FOMO (fear of missing out) among consumers, driving them to act quickly to secure limited-time offers or exclusive products. By creating a sense of exclusivity through limited edition releases, VIP access, or invite-only events, businesses can cultivate a sense of anticipation and desire, prompting consumers to take action before it's too late.

- **Gratification and Instant Rewards:** In today's fast-paced world, consumers crave instant gratification and rewards for their actions. Marketers can leverage gamification, loyalty programs, and rewards-based incentives to create a sense of achievement and satisfaction, encouraging repeat purchases and driving customer engagement. Whether it's earning points, unlocking badges, or receiving personalized rewards, businesses can tap into consumers' desire for instant gratification to drive loyalty and engagement.

Neuromarketing: Exploring the Neuroscience of Consumer Behaviour

In the quest to understand the intricacies of consumer behavior, businesses are turning to neuromarketing—a field that combines neuroscience, psychology, and marketing to uncover the subconscious drivers of consumer decision-making. By peering into the inner workings of the brain, neuro-marketers aim to decode the neural processes that influence consumer preferences, perceptions, and purchasing decisions **(ALSHARIF, et. al., 2021).**

- **Brain Imaging Techniques:** Neuromarketers utilize advanced brain imaging techniques such as functional magnetic resonance imaging (fMRI), electroencephalography (EEG), and eye-tracking to study brain activity and cognitive responses in real-time. These technologies allow researchers to identify neural patterns associated with different stimuli, such as advertisements, product packaging, and brand logos, providing valuable insights into consumer preferences and reactions.

- **Emotion and Memory Formation:** Emotions play a pivotal role in consumer decision-making, influencing perceptions, preferences, and brand associations. Neuromarketing research has revealed that emotional stimuli activate key areas of the brain involved in memory formation, leading to stronger emotional connections and brand recall. By eliciting positive emotions and creating memorable experiences, marketers can enhance brand engagement and foster long-term loyalty.

- **Attention and Engagement**: Neuromarketers study attention and engagement levels by analyzing neural activity in response to marketing stimuli. Eye-tracking technology allows researchers to monitor visual attention and gaze patterns, providing insights into which elements of an advertisement or website capture consumers' attention most effectively. By optimizing design elements and content placement, marketers can maximize engagement and drive conversion rates.

- **Decision-Making Processes:** Neuromarketing sheds light on the neural mechanisms underlying consumer decision-making processes, revealing how factors such as risk perception, social influence, and reward anticipation influence choices. By understanding these cognitive processes, marketers can design persuasive messaging and offer that resonate with consumers' subconscious desires and motivations, leading to more favorable outcomes.

- **Brand Perception and Trust:** Neuromarketing research has uncovered the neural correlates of brand perception and trust, highlighting the importance of authenticity, consistency, and credibility in shaping consumer attitudes toward brands. By aligning brand messaging with consumers' values and beliefs, businesses can build trust and loyalty over time, fostering strong emotional connections and advocacy.

- **Ethical Considerations:** While neuromarketing offers valuable insights into consumer behavior, ethical considerations regarding privacy, consent, and manipulation must be carefully addressed. As technology continues to advance, businesses must uphold ethical standards and transparency in their neuromarketing practices to ensure consumer trust and integrity.

The Role of AI and Automation in Shaping Consumer Behavior

AI-Powered Marketing: Enhancing Customer Experience

Artificial Intelligence (AI) has revolutionized the field of marketing by enabling businesses to deliver personalized, data-driven experiences that resonate with consumers on a deeper level. From predictive analytics to chatbots and recommendation engines, AI-powered marketing technologies have transformed the way businesses engage with their audience, driving higher levels of customer satisfaction and loyalty **(Kumar, et. al., 2024).**

Table 4: Statistical Evaluation: Impact of AI-Powered Personalization on Customer Engagement

Experiment	Control Group (Without AI-Powered Personalization)	Test Group (With AI-Powered Personalization)	Improvement (%)
Email Campaign	Open Rate: 15% Conversion Rate: 2%	Open Rate: 25% Conversion Rate: 4%	+67% Open Rate, +100% Conversion Rate
Product Recommendations	Average Click-Through Rate: 3%	Average Click-Through Rate: 7%	+133% Click-Through Rate
Website Personalization	Average Time on Site: 2 minutes	Average Time on Site: 5 minutes	+150% Time on Site
Chatbot Interaction	Customer Satisfaction Score: 3.5/5	Customer Satisfaction Score: 4.5/5	+29% Customer Satisfaction

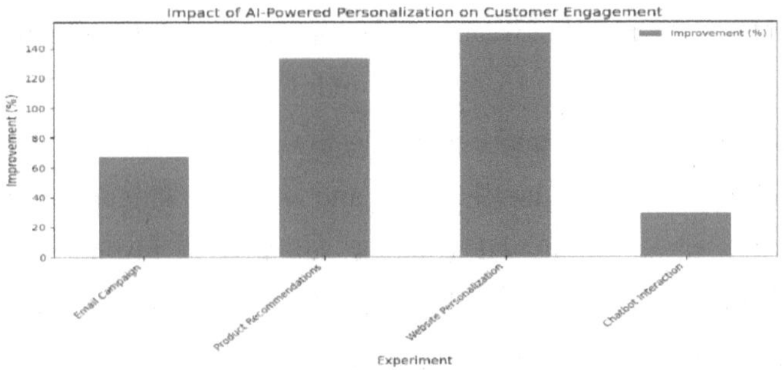

Figure 2: Visualization of the Impact of AI-Powered Personalization on Customer Engagement

In this scenario, the e-commerce retailer conducted a series of experiments comparing the performance of AI-powered personalization techniques against traditional marketing approaches. The control group represents customers who received standard marketing communications, while the test group received personalized recommendations and interactions powered by AI algorithms.

The statistical evaluation table demonstrates the significant improvements in customer engagement and conversion rates observed in the test group compared to the control group. From email campaigns and product recommendations to website personalization and chatbot interactions, AI-powered marketing strategies consistently outperformed traditional approaches, driving higher levels of engagement, satisfaction, and ultimately, conversion.

These results highlight the effectiveness of AI-powered marketing in enhancing the customer experience and driving business outcomes. By leveraging AI algorithms to analyze customer data, predict behavior, and deliver personalized experiences at scale, businesses can create more meaningful interactions that resonate with consumers and drive longterm loyalty and advocacy.

Chatbots and Virtual Assistants: Redefining Customer Interaction

In today's digital landscape, chatbots and virtual assistants have emerged as powerful tools for redefining customer interaction, streamlining processes, and enhancing the overall customer experience. Powered by artificial intelligence and natural language processing capabilities, these automated systems can provide instant responses to customer queries, offer personalized recommendations, and even facilitate transactions in real-time **(Ali, and A., 2024)**.

Table 5: Statistical Evaluation: Impact of Chatbots and Virtual Assistants on Customer Interaction

Metric	Before Implementation	After Implementation	Improvement (%)
Customer Satisfaction Score	3.8/5	4.5/5	+18%
Average Response Time	10 minutes	2 minutes	-80%
First Contact Resolution	60%	85%	+25%
Customer Retention Rate	80%	90%	+12.5%

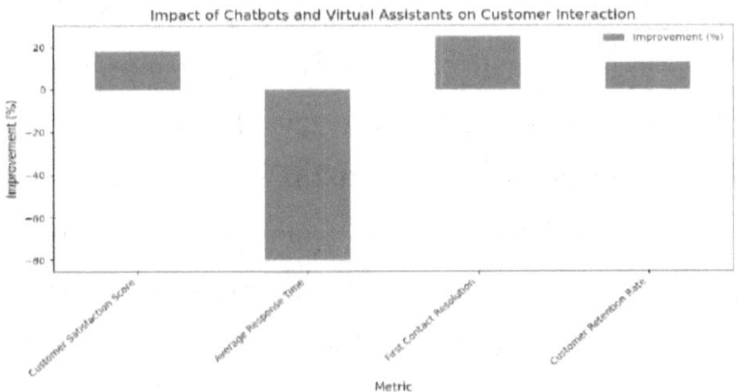

Figure 3: Visualization of the Impact of Chatbots and Virtual Assistants on Customer Interaction

In this case study, the telecommunications company implemented chatbots and virtual assistants to handle customer inquiries, technical support, and account management tasks. The statistical evaluation table compares key performance metrics before and after the implementation of these AI-powered systems.

The results clearly demonstrate the positive impact of chatbots and virtual assistants on customer interaction and service efficiency. Customer satisfaction scores improved by 18%, average response times decreased by 80%, first contact resolution rates increased by 25%, and customer retention rates grew by 12.5%.

These findings underscore the effectiveness of chatbots and virtual assistants in redefining customer interaction and delivering tangible business outcomes. By providing instant, personalized assistance round-the-clock, these AI-powered systems enhance convenience, efficiency, and satisfaction for customers while reducing operational costs and workload for businesses.

Ethical Considerations in AI-Driven Consumer Engagement

As businesses embrace AI and automation to enhance consumer engagement, it's essential to consider the ethical implications of these technologies. While AI-driven consumer engagement offers numerous benefits, including personalized experiences and improved efficiency, it also raises concerns related to privacy, fairness, transparency, and algorithmic bias **(Sheshadri, et. al., 2024)**.

- **Privacy Protection:** AI technologies often rely on vast amounts of consumer data to deliver personalized experiences. However, collecting and processing this data raises privacy concerns regarding the storage, usage, and security of personal information. Businesses must ensure compliance with data protection regulations such as GDPR and CCPA and implement robust security measures to safeguard consumer privacy.

- **Fairness and Transparency:** AI algorithms have the potential to perpetuate or exacerbate biases present in the training data, leading to unfair or discriminatory outcomes. Businesses must strive to develop and deploy AI systems that are transparent, accountable, and free from bias. This includes regularly auditing algorithms, mitigating bias in training data, and providing explanations for AI-driven decisions.

- **Informed Consent:** Consumers should have control over their data and how it's used for AI-driven engagement. Businesses must obtain informed consent from consumers before collecting, processing, or sharing their personal information for marketing purposes. This involves providing clear and concise disclosures about data practices and giving consumers the option to opt out or adjust privacy settings.

- **Algorithmic Governance:** Effective governance mechanisms are essential to ensure responsible AI use and mitigate potential risks. Businesses should establish ethical guidelines, codes of conduct, and oversight mechanisms to govern the development, deployment, and monitoring of AI systems. This includes appointing ethics committees, conducting impact assessments, and fostering a culture of responsible AI within the organization.

- **Accountability and Redress:** When AI-driven systems make mistakes or produce undesirable outcomes, businesses must take accountability and provide avenues for redress. This includes implementing complaint mechanisms, offering recourse for individuals affected by algorithmic decisions, and being transparent about corrective actions taken to address issues and prevent recurrence.

Navigating Cultural and Global Consumer Trends

Cultural Sensitivity in Marketing to Diverse Consumer Groups

In an increasingly interconnected world, businesses must navigate cultural diversity with sensitivity and nuance when marketing to diverse consumer groups. Cultural sensitivity entails understanding and respecting the values, beliefs, customs, and preferences of different cultural communities to create marketing campaigns that resonate authentically and respectfully **(Pires, et. al., 2000)**.

- **Cultural Research and Understanding:** Before targeting a specific cultural group, businesses must conduct thorough research to understand their values, traditions, language, and communication preferences. This includes studying cultural norms, historical context, religious practices, and societal taboos to ensure that marketing messages are appropriate and respectful.

- **Localization and Adaptation:** One-size-fits-all marketing approaches often fall short in diverse cultural landscapes. Businesses should tailor their marketing strategies to resonate with the cultural nuances and preferences of different consumer groups. This may involve adapting messaging, imagery, colors, and symbols to align with local customs and sensibilities.

- **Inclusive Representation:** Representation matters in marketing. Businesses should strive to reflect the diversity of their target audience in their marketing materials by featuring people from different ethnicities, backgrounds, ages, genders, and abilities. Inclusive representation not only fosters a sense of belonging but also attracts diverse consumer segments and builds brand loyalty.

- **Language and Communication:** Language plays a critical role in effective communication. Businesses should use culturally appropriate language and dialects to connect with diverse consumer groups. This may involve translating marketing materials into multiple languages, using idiomatic expressions, and considering linguistic nuances to ensure clarity and resonance.

- **Cultural Sensitivity Training:** Marketers and advertising professionals should undergo cultural sensitivity training to enhance their awareness and understanding of diverse cultural perspectives. Training programs can provide insights into cultural differences, implicit biases, and best practices for engaging with diverse audiences sensitively and effectively.

- **Community Engagement and Collaboration:** Building relationships with cultural communities requires genuine engagement and collaboration. Businesses should actively seek input, feedback, and partnership opportunities from community leaders, influencers, and organizations to co-create culturally relevant marketing initiatives that resonate authentically with their target audience.

By embracing cultural sensitivity in marketing, businesses can foster inclusivity, build trust, and cultivate meaningful connections with diverse consumer groups. By recognizing and respecting cultural diversity, businesses can unlock new market opportunities, drive brand loyalty, and create a positive social impact in an increasingly globalized world.

Globalization and its Impact on Consumer Behavior

Globalization has profoundly reshaped consumer behavior, creating a dynamic and interconnected marketplace where cultural boundaries blur and consumer preferences converge. The impact of globalization on consumer behavior is multifaceted, influencing everything from purchasing decisions and brand preferences to consumption patterns and cultural norms **(Rajagopal, and Rajagopal., 2013)**.

- **Access to Global Markets:** Advances in technology and transportation have facilitated greater access to products and services from around the world. Consumers can now shop online and access goods from distant markets with ease, leading to a proliferation of global brands and an increase in cross-border trade.

- **Cultural Homogenization:** Globalization has led to the spread of Western culture and values to diverse regions of the world, resulting in cultural homogenization in some areas. As a result, consumer preferences and consumption patterns become more standardized, with Western brands and lifestyles exerting influence on local markets.

- **Diversification of Consumer Preferences:** While globalization has led to cultural homogenization in some aspects, it has also sparked a counter-trend of cultural diversification. As consumers are exposed to a wider range of cultural influences and experiences, their preferences become more eclectic and diverse, leading to a demand for niche products and customization options.

- **Rise of Global Brands:** Globalization has enabled the rise of multinational corporations and global brands that operate across multiple countries and regions. These brands leverage economies of scale, sophisticated marketing strategies, and standardized product offerings to appeal to diverse consumer segments worldwide.

- **Shift towards Ethical Consumption:** Globalization has heightened awareness of social and environmental issues, prompting consumers to demand more ethical and sustainable products and practices from businesses. As consumers become more socially conscious, they prioritize factors such as corporate social responsibility, fair labor practices, and environmental sustainability in their purchasing decisions.

- **Emergence of Cross-Cultural Marketing:** In response to the complexities of global consumer behavior, businesses are adopting cross-cultural marketing strategies that recognize and celebrate cultural diversity. Rather than imposing a one-size-fits-all approach, these strategies embrace cultural nuances and adapt marketing messages to resonate authentically with diverse audiences.

Overall, globalization has transformed consumer behavior in profound ways, reshaping the way people shop, consume, and interact with brands in an increasingly interconnected world. By understanding the complexities of global consumer trends and adapting their strategies accordingly, businesses can thrive in the global marketplace and build meaningful connections with diverse audiences across cultures and borders.

Adapting Marketing Strategies to Localized Consumer Preferences

In today's globalized marketplace, successful businesses recognize the importance of adapting their marketing strategies to resonate with localized consumer preferences. While globalization has led to cultural convergence in some aspects, consumers across different regions and markets still exhibit unique preferences, behaviors, and cultural nuances that must be considered when developing marketing campaigns **(Okonkwo, et. al., 2023).**

- **Market Research and Localization:** Conduct thorough market research to understand the cultural, social, and economic factors that influence consumer behavior in specific regions. This includes studying language, customs, traditions, and consumer trends to tailor marketing messages and campaigns to resonate with local audiences effectively.

- **Customization and Personalization:** Embrace customization and personalization to meet the diverse needs and preferences of local consumers. This may involve adapting product offerings, pricing strategies, and promotional tactics to align with local tastes, preferences, and purchasing habits.

- **Cultural Sensitivity and Respect:** Show respect for local customs, values, and traditions in marketing communications. Avoid cultural stereotypes, insensitive imagery, or messaging that may offend or alienate local audiences. Instead, celebrate cultural diversity and embrace authenticity to build trust and rapport with consumers.

- **Localization of Content and Messaging:** Translate marketing materials, website content, and advertising campaigns into the local language(s) to improve accessibility and comprehension for local audiences. Additionally, adapt visual elements, colors, and symbols to align with cultural norms and preferences.

- **Engagement with Local Communities:** Build relationships with local communities by engaging with influencers, community leaders, and cultural organizations. Seek input and feedback from local stakeholders to co-create marketing initiatives that resonate authentically with the target audience.

- **Flexibility and Adaptability:** Be flexible and adaptable in response to changing market dynamics and consumer preferences. Monitor local trends, gather feedback from customers, and adjust marketing strategies accordingly to stay relevant and competitive in local markets.

By adapting marketing strategies to localized consumer preferences, businesses can foster stronger connections with local audiences, drive brand loyalty, and achieve sustainable growth in diverse markets. By recognizing and respecting the uniqueness of each market, businesses can position themselves as trusted partners and valuable contributors to the communities they serve.

Future-proofing Marketing and Management Strategies

Agility and Adaptability: Key Traits for Future Success

In an era of rapid technological advancement and evolving consumer preferences, agility and adaptability are paramount for future-proofing marketing and management strategies. Businesses must embrace a mindset of continuous learning, experimentation, and innovation to stay ahead of the curve and thrive in an ever-changing landscape.

- **Navigating Uncertainty and Disruption:** The business landscape is increasingly characterized by uncertainty, volatility, and disruption. Agile organizations can quickly pivot and adapt to changing market conditions, emerging trends, and unexpected challenges, enabling them to seize opportunities and mitigate risks more effectively.

- **Meeting Changing Consumer Expectations:** Consumer

preferences and behaviors are constantly evolving in response to technological advancements, cultural shifts, and global events. Agile businesses can anticipate and respond to these changes by listening to customer feedback, analyzing market trends, and iterating their products, services, and marketing strategies accordingly.

- **Innovation and Experimentation:** Agility fosters a culture of innovation and experimentation, where employees are empowered to test new ideas, take calculated risks, and learn from failures. By encouraging a growth mindset and embracing a willingness to adapt, businesses can drive continuous improvement and stay ahead of the competition.

- **Flexibility in Strategy Execution:** Agile organizations adopt flexible and iterative approaches to strategy execution, allowing them to adjust course as needed based on real-time feedback and market insights. This iterative approach enables businesses to course-correct, experiment with new tactics, and optimize performance in pursuit of strategic objectives.

- **Resilience in Times of Change:** The ability to adapt quickly is essential for resilience in times of change or crisis. Agile businesses can respond nimbly to unexpected disruptions, such as economic downturns, supply chain disruptions, or global pandemics, by re-evaluating priorities, reallocating resources, and innovating new solutions to overcome challenges.

- **Continuous Learning and Growth**: Agility and adaptability require a commitment to continuous learning and growth at both the individual and organizational levels. By fostering a culture of curiosity, collaboration, and self-improvement, businesses can equip their teams with the skills, knowledge, and mindset needed to navigate complexity and thrive in a rapidly changing environment.

Innovation in Marketing and Management Practices

Innovation is the lifeblood of progress, driving continuous improvement and transformation in marketing and management practices. As businesses navigate an increasingly complex and competitive landscape, embracing innovation is essential for staying ahead of the curve, meeting evolving consumer needs, and driving sustainable growth **(Garrido-Moreno, et. al., 2015)**.

- **Meeting Changing Consumer Demands:** Innovation allows businesses to develop new products, services, and experiences that address changing consumer needs and preferences. By staying attuned to market trends, harnessing emerging technologies, and fostering a culture of creativity, businesses can deliver innovative solutions that resonate with customers and differentiate themselves from competitors.

- **Enhancing Customer Experience:** Innovation in marketing and management practices enables businesses to deliver exceptional customer experiences that delight and engage consumers at every touchpoint. Whether through personalized marketing campaigns, seamless omnichannel experiences, or innovative product features, businesses can create memorable interactions that foster loyalty and advocacy

- **Driving Efficiency and Effectiveness:** Innovative management practices leverage automation, data analytics, and process optimization to drive efficiency and effectiveness across the organization. By streamlining workflows, eliminating bottlenecks, and leveraging technology to automate routine tasks, businesses can optimize resource allocation, reduce costs, and improve overall performance.

- **Promoting Collaboration and Creativity:** Innovation thrives in environments that foster collaboration, diversity of thought, and a willingness to experiment. By creating cross-functional teams, encouraging open communication, and empowering employees to contribute ideas, businesses can harness the collective intelligence of their workforce to drive innovation and problem-solving.

- **Adapting to Technological Advancements:** Rapid advancements in technology, such as artificial intelligence, machine learning, and augmented reality, present opportunities for innovation in marketing and management practices. By embracing emerging technologies and exploring new possibilities, businesses can unlock innovative solutions that drive competitive advantage and position them for future success.

- **Embracing a Growth Mindset:** Innovation requires a mindset of continuous learning, adaptation, and resilience. By embracing a growth mindset and viewing challenges as opportunities for growth and innovation, businesses can cultivate a culture of innovation that empowers employees to think creatively, take calculated risks, and drive positive change.

Strategies for Anticipating and Responding to Future Trends

In a rapidly evolving business environment, the ability to anticipate and respond to future trends is crucial for staying ahead of the competition and driving sustainable growth. By proactively identifying emerging opportunities and challenges, businesses can position themselves to capitalize on new market dynamics and adapt their strategies accordingly.

- **Market Research and Trend Analysis:** Conduct comprehensive market research and trend analysis to identify emerging opportunities and threats in your industry. Stay informed about market dynamics, consumer preferences, technological advancements, and regulatory changes that may impact your business. Leverage data analytics, market intelligence tools, and industry reports to gain insights into future trends and anticipate shifts in the competitive landscape.

- **Scenario Planning and Risk Management:** Develop scenario planning exercises to anticipate various future scenarios and assess their potential impact on your business. Identify key drivers of change, such as technological disruptions, economic shifts, or geopolitical events, and evaluate their implications for your organization. Implement risk management strategies to mitigate potential threats and capitalize on opportunities presented by future trends.

- **Strategic Partnerships and Alliances:** Form strategic partnerships and alliances with industry stakeholders, technology providers, startups, and research institutions to stay abreast of emerging trends and innovation opportunities. Collaborate with external partners to co-create solutions, share knowledge, and leverage complementary strengths that enable your business to respond effectively to future trends.

- **Investment in Innovation and R&D:** Allocate resources to invest in innovation and research and development (R&D) initiatives that drive long-term growth and competitiveness. Foster a culture of innovation within your organization by encouraging experimentation, rewarding creativity, and supporting cross-functional collaboration. Embrace emerging technologies, such as artificial intelligence, blockchain, and Internet of Things (IoT), to develop innovative products, services, and business models that anticipate future trends.

- **Agility and Flexibility in Strategy Execution:** Develop agile and flexible strategic planning processes that enable your organization to quickly adapt to changing market conditions and customer preferences. Implement iterative approaches to strategy execution, such as agile project management methodologies, that allow for rapid experimentation, learning, and adjustment based on feedback and performance metrics.

- **Continuous Learning and Development:** Invest in continuous learning and development initiatives to equip your workforce with the skills, knowledge, and capabilities needed to navigate future trends successfully. Provide training programs, workshops, and mentorship opportunities that empower employees to stay current with industry trends, develop new competencies, and embrace lifelong learning as a core value.

Conclusion

In this book chapter, we have explored the futuristic trends in marketing and management, focusing on the dynamic landscape of consumer behavior. We began by examining the rapid evolution of consumer behavior, driven by technological advancements, cultural shifts, and changing market dynamics. From there, we delved into the intersection of technology and consumer behavior, highlighting the importance of understanding future trends in marketing and management.

We discussed the emergence of the digital consumer landscape, shifts in consumer preferences and expectations, and the impact of technology on consumer decision-making processes. We also explored the role of data-driven insights and predictive analytics in understanding consumer behavior, as well as the psychological aspects that influence consumer decision-making.

Furthermore, we examined the role of AI and automation in shaping consumer behavior, emphasizing the importance of AI-powered marketing in enhancing customer experience. We discussed chatbots and virtual assistants' role in redefining customer interaction and the ethical considerations in AI-driven consumer engagement.

Additionally, we explored navigating cultural and global consumer trends, emphasizing the importance of cultural sensitivity in marketing to diverse consumer groups and adapting marketing strategies to localized consumer preferences.

Finally, we discussed future-proofing marketing and management strategies, focusing on agility, adaptability, innovation, and strategies for anticipating and responding to future trends.

As we look ahead, it is clear that the future of consumer behavior will be shaped by technological innovation, cultural diversity, and evolving consumer expectations. Businesses that embrace these opportunities and adapt their strategies accordingly will be well-positioned to succeed in the rapidly changing marketplace. By leveraging emerging technologies, fostering a culture of innovation, and staying attuned to evolving consumer needs, businesses can drive sustainable growth and create meaningful connections with their audience.

In conclusion, we urge businesses to embrace change and innovation in marketing and management. The future belongs to those who are willing to adapt, innovate, and embrace new possibilities. By staying agile, responsive, and forward-thinking, businesses can navigate uncertainty, seize opportunities, and thrive in an ever-changing world. Let us commit to embracing change, fostering innovation, and shaping the future of consumer behavior through our collective efforts in marketing and management.

As we embark on this journey together, let us remember that the future is ours to shape, and by embracing change and innovation, we can create a brighter tomorrow for businesses and consumers alike.

References

1. ALSHARIF, A. H., SALLEH, N. Z. M., Baharun, R. O. H. A. I. Z. A. T., & YUSOFF, M. E. (2021). Consumer behaviour through neuromarketing approach. The journal of contemporary issues in business and government, 27(3), 344-354.

2. Ameen, N., Hosany, S., & Tarhini, A. (2021). Consumer interaction with cutting-edge technologies: Implications for future research. Computers in Human Behavior, 120, 106761.

3. Barroso, M., & Laborda, J. (2022). Digital transformation and the emergence of the Fintech sector: Systematic literature review. Digital Business, 2(2), 100028.

4. Chandra, S., Verma, S., Lim, W. M., Kumar, S., & Donthu, N. (2022). Personalization in personalized marketing: Trends and ways forward. Psychology & Marketing, 39(8), 1529- Ali, A. (2024). Revolutionizing Customer Support: the Impact of AI-Powered Chatbots and Virtual Assistants (No. 12037). EasyChair.

5. Chaudhry, U. B., & Chaudhry, M. A. (2023, January). Harnessing big data for business innovation and effective business decision making. In Cybersecurity in the Age of Smart Societies: Proceedings of the 14th International Conference on Global Security, Safety and Sustainability, London, September 2022 (pp. 47-60). Cham: Springer International Publishing.

6. Cleveland, M., Laroche, M., & Takahashi, I. (2015). The intersection of global consumer culture and national identity and the effect on Japanese consumer behavior. Journal of International Consumer Marketing, 27(5), 364-387.

7. Dahake, P. S., Bagaregari, P., & Dahake, N. S. (2024). Shaping the Future of Retail: A Comprehensive Review of Predictive Analytics Models for Consumer Behavior. Entrepreneurship and Creativity in the Metaverse, 143-160.

8. Dixit, A. (2020). Emotional Design: Utilizing Emotional Triggers to Influence Consumer Behaviour. Eduzone: International Peer Reviewed/Refereed Multidisciplinary Journal, 9(1), 19-28.

9. Elena, P. M., Loredana, U. E., Carmen, M. A., Elena, P. E., & Alexandra, J. (2021). Consumer preferences and expectations.

Trends in Wheat and Bread Making, 431-458.

10. Erevelles, S., Fukawa, N., & Swayne, L. (2016). Big Data consumer analytics and the transformation of marketing. Journal of business research, 69(2), 897-904.

11. Fetene, G. M., Kaplan, S., Mabit, S. L., Jensen, A. F., & Prato, C. G. (2017). Harnessing big data for estimating the energy consumption and driving range of electric vehicles. Transportation Research Part D: Transport and Environment, 54, 1-11.

12. Garrido-Moreno, A., Lockett, N., & Garcia-Morales, V. (2015). Exploring the role of knowledge management practices in fostering customer relationship management as a catalyst of marketing innovation. Baltic Journal of Management, 10(4), 393-412.

13. Korteling, J. E., Paradies, G. L., & Sassen-van Meer, J. P. (2023). Cognitive bias and how to improve sustainable decision making. Frontiers in Psychology, 14, 1129835.

14. Kumar, V., Ashraf, A. R., & Nadeem, W. (2024). AI-powered marketing: What, where, and how?. International Journal of Information Management, 102783.

15. Mogaji, E., & Nguyen, N. P. (2024). Evaluating the emergence of contactless digital payment technology for transportation. Technological Forecasting and Social Change, 203, 123378.

16. Naim, A. (2022). New Trends in Marketing Management: Conceptual Framework. American Journal of Business Management, Economics and Banking, 4, 14-26.

17. Okonkwo, I., Mujinga, J., Namkoisse, E., & Francisco, A. (2023). Localization and Global Marketing: Adapting Digital Strategies for Diverse Audiences. Journal of Digital Marketing and Communication, 3(2), 66-80.

18. Parc, J., & Kim, S. D. (2020). The digital transformation of the Korean music industry and the global emergence of K-pop.

Sustainability, 12(18), 7790.

19. Peck, J., & Shu, S. B. (Eds.). (2018). Psychological ownership and consumer behavior. Springer.

20. Pires, G., & Stanton, J. (2000). Marketing services to ethnic consumers in culturally diverse markets: issues and implications. Journal of Services Marketing, 14(7), 607-618.

21. Rajagopal, & Rajagopal. (2013). Globalization and Consumer Behavior. Managing Social Media and Consumerism: The Grapevine Effect in Competitive Markets, 217-229.

22. Raji, M. A., Olodo, H. B., Oke, T. T., Addy, W. A., Ofodile, O. C., & Oyewole, A. T. (2024). E-commerce and consumer behavior: A review of AI-powered personalization and market trends. GSC Advanced Research and Reviews, 18(3), 066-077.

23. Sharma, P., Ueno, A., Dennis, C., & Turan, C. P. (2023). Emerging digital technologies and consumer decision-making in retail sector: Towards an integrative conceptual framework. Computers in Human Behavior, 148, 107913.

24. Sheshadri, T., Shelly, R., Sharma, K., Sharma, T., & Basha, M. (2024). An Empirical Study on Integration of Artificial Intelligence and Marketing Management to Transform Consumer Engagement in Selected PSU Banks (PNB and Canara Banks). Naturalista campano, 28(1), 463-4711562.

25. Vidhya, V., Donthu, S., Veeran, L., Lakshmi, Y. S., & Yadav, B. (2023). The intersection of AI and consumer behavior: Predictive models in modern marketing. Remittances Review, 8(4).

26. Zhou, X., Liu, H., Li, J., Zhang, K., & Lev, B. (2023). Channel strategies when digital platforms emerge: A systematic literature review. Omega, 102919.

A Study on Marketing Strategies of Health Insurance Companies in Business Development in Delhi Region

✍ Dr. Tarun Chauhan

Abstract

After conducting a comprehensive analysis of health insurance marketing strategies and survey outcomes, this study will assess the impact of these strategies on increasing the penetration of health insurance schemes and enhancing consumer awareness, particularly in the Delhi region. The study will also evaluate the challenges related to data availability and sharing, proposing measures for improvement. The survey analysis will assist health insurance companies in addressing transparency issues and developing suitable recommendations to build trust, confidence, and a positive image among customers. The report will also offer suggestions for improving service quality, customer retention, product differentiation, and pricing strategies for health insurance companies.

Keywords: Marketting, strategy, Health Insurance, Business development and company

Introduction

The healthcare sector is one of the largest contributors to India's economy, both in terms of revenue generation and employment opportunities. It is experiencing significant growth due to increased coverage, improved services, and rising investments from both public and private sectors. In the Union Budget 2023-24, the Ministry of Health and Family Welfare has been allocated INR 89,155 crore, marking a 3.43% increase from INR 86,200.65 crore in 2021-22.

India's approach to health insurance penetration is highly decentralized. Health insurance remains optional in India, and a significant portion of the population ends up using a substantial portion of their savings to cover increasing healthcare costs due to inadequate insurance coverage.

Health insurance coverage in India is far from satisfactory. According to data from the National Family Health Survey India report (2022), only 41% of households have at least one usual member covered by health insurance. Specifically, between 2019-2021, only 30% of women aged 15-49 and 33% of men aged 15-49 are covered by health insurance or financing schemes. Nearly half (46%) of those with insurance are covered by state health insurance schemes, and about one-sixth (16%) are covered by the Rashtriya Swasthya Bima Yojana (RSBY). A small percentage, approximately 3-6% of women and 4-7% of men, are covered by the Employee State Insurance Scheme (ESIS) or the Central Government Health Scheme (CGHS). The highest percentage of households covered under health insurance or financing schemes is found in Rajasthan (88%) and Andhra Pradesh (80%), while the lowest coverage (less than 15%) is in the Andaman & Nicobar Islands and Jammu & Kashmir.

The health insurance market in India is growing, but the distribution of health insurance policies is uneven. Additionally, the public healthcare system faces challenges due to inadequate funding, leading most Indians to opt for private health insurance providers known for their superior and prompt services.

Compared to global healthcare costs in countries like the US, Canada, the UK, Japan, and Russia, India's healthcare costs are significantly lower. While the Indian health insurance industry has numerous players, it still offers substantial opportunities for new companies. Foreign insurance companies operate in India through joint ventures, and they must follow proper regulatory procedures to establish a presence in the market.

In a narrow sense, health insurance involves individuals or groups purchasing healthcare coverage in advance by paying a premium. In a broader context, it encompasses any arrangement that helps individuals and households defer, delay, reduce, or avoid healthcare expenses. In the Indian context, this broader definition is more appropriate, considering that health insurance coverage in India is limited, covering only about 10% of the total population. The existing schemes can be categorized into voluntary health insurance schemes (private-for-profit), employer-based schemes, insurance offered by NGOs/community-based health insurance, and mandatory health insurance schemes (government-run schemes such as ESIS and CGHS).

Health Insurance Marketing Strategies Overview

India, as a nation, has a low level of insurance coverage, both in urban and rural areas. Only 35% of the 250 million individuals who could potentially be insured have insurance. To enhance insurance penetration, insurance companies should explore new segments, particularly the relatively untapped rural market, instead of competing for a share of the same market in urban areas. Therefore, insurance companies have ample opportunities to expand their presence in both urban and rural India. This research aims to identify a range of suggestions for segmentation, pricing, and customer retention strategies that can assist health insurance companies in attracting more customers and retaining their existing ones for longer periods.

Need of the Study

India is grappling with a significant burden of lifestyle diseases like heart problems, diabetes, and respiratory ailments. While these conditions are treatable in India, the costs associated with their treatment have skyrocketed. This increase in costs is attributed to advancements in medical research and the use of sophisticated medical technologies. India witnesses approximately 5.8 million deaths each year due to non-communicable diseases (NCDs).

According to the MMB Health Trends report for 2023, the top drivers of medical claims in Asia in 2021 were cancer (55%), diseases related to the circulatory system (43%), and Covid-19 (36%). Among these, respiratory diseases (47%), gastrointestinal diseases (36%), and Covid-19 (34%) had the highest frequency of claims. Recent data from the Niti Aayog Report (2021) suggests that the existing health insurance schemes in India have the potential to cover only around 95 crore individuals. These schemes encompass government-subsidized, social health insurance, and private insurance programs.

With the changing lifestyles and the escalating costs of healthcare, acquiring health insurance coverage has become a necessity rather than a luxury. Given this context, health insurance policies offer a crucial means of preparation for unforeseen medical expenses. Therefore, this study primarily focuses on understanding the current marketing strategies employed by private and public health insurance companies in the Delhi region. Given the state of health insurance in India, it is imperative to urgently implement effective marketing strategies in the Delhi region to promote health insurance coverage.

Objectives of the Study

The primary aim of this study is to comprehend the current marketing strategies employed by both private and public health insurance companies operating in the Delhi region.

1. To ascertain the underlying causes for the limited adoption of health insurance schemes, particularly in the Delhi region.

2. To investigate the factors contributing to the low level of consumer awareness regarding health insurance products and their advantages, and to propose effective measures to enhance awareness among urban, sub-urban, and rural consumers.

3. To examine the challenges associated with an inadequate retail distribution model and a lack of transparency in the industry. Additionally, to offer recommendations for fortifying the retail distribution network and establishing trust, confidence, and a positive image among customers.

4. To address the issues faced by health insurance companies, including customer retention, product differentiation, and pricing. Furthermore, to assess and extract expert recommendations for formulating robust marketing strategies for these companies.

5. To pinpoint the factors that hinder the purchase of health insurance policies.

6. To establish the correlation between socio-demographic variables and the low adoption and awareness levels of health insurance schemes.

Hypothesis-Testing

H1: A noteworthy correlation exists between the limited adoption and certain socio-demographic variables.

H2: A substantial correlation is evident between the reduced awareness levels and specific socio-demographic variables.

Scope of the Study

The study's scope encompasses surveying consumers in urban, semi-urban, and rural areas within the Delhi Region. Its primary focus is to shed light on the services provided by health insurance companies. Additionally, the study aims to illuminate the current marketing strategies employed by both public and private insurance providers in the Delhi Region, with a particular emphasis on schemes implemented from 2020 onwards.

Review of Literature

Since the liberalization of the insurance industry, the health insurance sector in India has gained substantial importance both economically and socially. Researchers have delved into various facets of this sector:

1. Aubu (2014) conducted a comparative study on the marketing strategies of health insurance policies between public and private companies. The study revealed that private sector companies garnered a more favorable response due to their adoption of innovative strategies and technologies.

2. Alireza Miremadi (2011) highlighted the connection between market research, surveys, and media in the insurance industry. These tools assist insurance companies' advertising managers in selecting the most effective media combinations to reach potential customers.

3. Binny and Gupta (2017) explored the opportunities and challenges within the Indian health insurance landscape. While opportunities exist for market expansion, companies grapple with structural issues such as high claim ratios and evolving customer needs, necessitating product innovation.

4. Charkravarti (2006) reported that individuals below the poverty line struggle to afford health insurance premiums, and insurance agents often lack proper policy knowledge. Many in the general public rely on financial assistance from neighbors and communities to bear the burden of medical expenses.

5. Chatterjee et al. (2018) investigated the state of the health-care insurance industry in India, emphasizing the country's focus on short-term care and the need to transition toward long-term care.

6. Chauhan (2019) examined the intricacies of medical underwriting and rating modalities in the health insurance sector. It was revealed

that underwriting a health policy involves considering various aspects of the insured, including lifestyle, occupation, health condition, and habits.

7. Dror et al. (2006) studied the willingness of rural and economically disadvantaged individuals in India to pay for health insurance. The study found that insured individuals were more willing to pay for their insurance compared to the uninsured.

8. Gambhir et al. (2019) analyzed the coverage of outpatient care by private sector insurance in India, noting a considerable increase in the share of private health insurance companies despite challenges in the sector.

9. Kumar (2009) explored the role of insurance in financing healthcare in India, emphasizing the potential of insurance to mobilize resources and provide risk protection and health facilities, while also highlighting the need for systemic reforms.

10. Mahal (2003) assessed the potential impact of private players entering the health insurance market in India. The analysis suggested that with relaxed entry conditions, the health insurance market could surpass the existing business of General Insurance Companies of India, with equity-enhancing effects, including reduced use of public sector hospitalization facilities by higher-income groups.

11. Nair (2019) conducted a comparative study of the satisfaction levels of health insurance claimants with public and private sector general insurance companies. The study found relatively higher satisfaction with claim settlement in the public sector.

12. Thomas (2017) examined health insurance in India from a consumer insights perspective, highlighting factors considered by consumers when selecting a health insurer, such as the availability of a robust hospital network, policy coverage, product choices, and responsive

customer service.

13. Savita (2014) investigated the reasons behind the declining membership of micro health insurance in Karnataka, attributing the decline to financial constraints, lack of clarity about the scheme, and intra-household factors. Designing schemes that cater to customer needs emerged as a central challenge in the microinsurance sector.

14. Shah (2017) analysed the health insurance sector in India post-liberalization, revealing a significant relationship between premiums collected, claims paid, and demographic variables affecting policy holding status.

15. Vinod and Saharan (2007) noted a growing awareness among the general public regarding the benefits and importance of health insurance in today's world. They observed a continuous increase in premium levels and the growth index of the health insurance business in India. Public sector players saw a decline in their market share in health insurance, while private sector players witnessed growth in their contributions.

16. Wouter Langenhoff (2008) emphasized the health insurance industry's focus on service quality and the importance of considering switching costs in customer retention. Customer satisfaction, as the core offering of health insurers, played a pivotal role in retaining customers.

17. Yadav and Sudhakar (2017) studied the personal factors influencing the purchase decisions of health insurance policies in India. Their findings highlighted the significant influence of factors such as awareness, tax benefits, financial security, and risk coverage on the purchase decisions of health insurance policyholders.

Theoretical Framework

This study was based on the following theories from which the variables for analyzed were derived from:

- Resource Dependence Theory

Pfeffer and Salancik (1978) drew upon existing environmental literature to formulate the theory of resource dependence. This theory is founded on the concept that organizations rely on their external environments as the primary source of limited resources crucial for their survival. When organizations lack control over these resources, it introduces uncertainty into their operations. To ensure their survival, organizations must devise strategies for acquiring and utilizing these resources, which are often sought after by other firms. This theory emerged from the recognition that organizations cannot solely generate all the resources they require internally. Consequently, they must engage in external agreements and transactions to secure additional resources, giving them a competitive advantage. Pfeffer and Salancik (1978) identified three factors that determined the extent to which organizations depended on specific resources. The first factor was the overall significance of the resource to the organization, which played a critical role in determining resource dependence. Second, the scarcity of the resource was another influential factor; the scarcer a resource, the more dependent the organization became. Lastly, competition among organizations for control of a particular resource also played a role in influencing resource dependence. Together, these three factors collectively determined the level of an organization's dependence on a specific resource.

- Commitment Trust Theory

The commitment-trust theory asserts that for a relationship to thrive, it necessitates the presence of two essential elements: trust and commitment (Cook, Karen & Richard, 1978). Day (1970) proposed that strategic marketing revolves around establishing connections with customers, catering to their requirements, and honouring agreements. Rather than solely pursuing short-term profits, businesses that adhere to the principles of relationship marketing focus on cultivating enduring relationships with their customers. Consequently, these businesses gain the trust of their customers, and this mutual loyalty aids both parties in meeting their respective needs (Meyer & Natalie, 1984). Trust is rooted in the confidence shared between parties in a relationship. Typically, businesses foster trust by instilling confidence in their customers. Commitment involves a lasting commitment to maintaining a valuable partnership. This commitment drives businesses to continually invest in the development and sustenance of relationships with their customers.

- Resource Based View Theory

The resource-based view of the firm directs attention to the firm's internal environment as a primary driver of competitive advantage and underscores the significance of the resources a firm has cultivated to compete effectively in its surroundings (Armstrong, 2012). This theory was originally introduced by Penrose in 1959 and serves as a managerial framework for identifying the strategic resources capable of providing a competitive edge to a firm. Over time, the theory has shifted its focus from examining industry structure to analyzing the internal composition of firms, with resources and capabilities becoming the central elements of the resource-based view. Consequently, the resource-based view of strategy has gained prominence as a widely accepted strategic theory for achieving a competitive advantage (Brown, 2010). It underscores that the resources owned, employed, and harnessed by the organization hold more significance than the structure of the industry itself.

Influenced by Porter's studies in 1985, the concept of competitive advantage explains a firm's success concerning the characteristics of its industry sector. According to this perspective, firms operating within the same industry sector, facing similar opportunities and few, if any, distinctions between them, maintain their competitive positions for only a limited duration (Schweitzer, 2014). The resource-based view (RBV) represents a distinctive approach to understanding the firm and shaping its strategy. Essentially, this theory views the firm as an amalgamation of resources. It is the nature of these resources and how they are combined that sets firms apart from one another. This approach is often described as an inside-out analysis, where the starting point is an exploration of the organization's internal environment.

Research Methodology

This study relies on both primary and secondary data sources. Primary data will be gathered through personal interviews using questionnaires, along with structured and unstructured interviews to obtain firsthand insights related to the research theme. Data will be collected from both health insurance policyholders and non-policyholders in the Delhi Region.

In addition, secondary data will be sourced from a variety of outlets including journals, books, manuals, reports, magazines, business newspapers, and visits to health insurance companies and related institutions. Data collected from both primary and secondary sources will be analyzed using statistical tools.

- Research Design - The study adopts a Descriptive Research Design.
- Sampling Method - Convenient Sampling will be used. The researcher plans to visit eight health insurance companies: National Insurance, New India, Bajaj Allianz, HDFC Ergo, ICICI Lombard, Iffco Tokio, Max Bupa, and Star Health & Allied Insurance.
- Sample Size - The study aims to distribute 100 questionnaires to consumers of health insurance companies in the Delhi Region to achieve its research objectives, resulting in a total sample size of 150.
- Data Analysis Tools - Statistical tools including Descriptive statistics (Frequency/Percentage/Diagrams/Tabulation/Mean/Median/Mode/ Standard Deviation) and Inferential Statistics (Karl Pearson Correlation Test) will be employed. Additionally, two sets of

questionnaires concerning marketing strategies and issues faced by insurers and consumers will be used.

- Pilot Testing - After designing the two sets of questionnaires for health insurance companies, a pilot testing study will be conducted to ensure they yield the desired results.
- Reliability - The internal consistency of the measurement scale will be tested using Cronbach's alpha. A Cronbach's alpha value above 0.7 indicates scale reliability.

Relevance of the Study

The study's population consists of all health insurance policyholders and non-policyholders in the Delhi region. Non-policyholders will be considered to assess their potential interest in health insurance policy schemes. The study will delve into the literature on health insurance schemes, analyze customer feedback regarding awareness and service quality, and gather data on existing schemes and marketing strategies through visits to both public and private health insurance companies. Customer-related data, including policyholder records, customer feedback forms, and sales performance data, will be collected and evaluated. Following the evaluation process, recommendations will be developed to enhance the marketing strategies of health insurance companies.

Limitations of the Study

a) The study is confined to the Delhi region.
b) Limitations include potential issues related to illiteracy, unresponsiveness, and unwillingness.
c) The study focuses solely on the marketing strategies of health insurance.
d) It is also restricted to a selection of private and public health insurance companies.

Conclusion

After conducting a comprehensive analysis of health insurance marketing strategies and survey outcomes, this study will assess the impact of these strategies on increasing the penetration of health insurance schemes and enhancing consumer awareness, particularly in the Delhi region. The study will also evaluate the challenges related to data availability and sharing, proposing measures for improvement. The survey analysis will assist health insurance companies in addressing transparency issues and developing suitable recommendations to build trust, confidence, and a positive image among customers. The report will also offer suggestions for improving service quality, customer retention, product differentiation, and pricing strategies for health insurance companies.

References

1. Bhat Ramesh & Mavlankar Dileep (2000) 'Health insurance in India Opportunities, Challenges and Concerns', IIM, Ahmadabad. Available   at https://www.researchgate.net/publication/238659220_Health_Insurance_in_India_Opportunities_Challenges_and_Concerns

2. Thakur Anand, BS Hundal, (2006). "Rural Consumer: A Opportunity Beyond Saturated Markets". The ICFAI Journal of Marketing Management, 6 (1), 27-34.

3. Ramaswamy, V.S. and S Namakumari (2004). "Marketing Management planning, Implementation and Control (3rd Edition). New Delhi. Macmillan, 262-277.

4. Richard Holloway and Rajagopalan Krishnamurthy. (2006). "Insuring rural India". Journal of Insurance Chronicle, 6(12), 47-51.

5. L.P.Gupta, (2008). "Social Security in India", Insurance Chronicle, The ICFAI University Press, 8(6) 17-21.

6. Kumar Anurag, and Sarwal Rakesh (2021). "Health Insurance for India's Missing Middle" (ISBN:978-81-949510-2-5),

NITIAayog,1-48   https://www.niti.gov.in/sites/default/files/2023-02/Health-Insurance-for-India%E2%80%99s-Missing-Middle_08-12-2021.pdf

7. National Health Family Survey (2019-2021). "COMPENDIUM OF FACT SHEETS INDIA AND 14 STATES/UTs (Phase-11)", Ministry of health and family welfare, government of India, 22-116. https://main.mohfw.gov.in/sites/default/files/NFHS-5_Phase-II_0.pdf

8. Siddharth Mandrekar Rao (2023). "Demand for Grants 2023-24 Analysis: Health and Family Welfare", PRS Legislative Research, 1-17. https://prsindia.org/files/budget/budget_parliament/2023/DfG_2023-24-Health_and_Family_Welfare.pdf

9. Global insurer survey report. MMB health trends 2023: Navigating cost trends and using innovation in employer-provided healthcare, 1-46. https://www.euro-center.com/wp-content/uploads/2023/04/gl-2023-mmb-health-trends-global-report.pdf

10. Raj Kumar Singh (2017). "Study on Marketing Strategies of Health Insurance Companies in Nagpur region", International Journal of Research in Business Studies, 2 (1), 153-160.

11. Aubu, R. (2014). "Marketing of health insurance policies: a comparative study on public and private insurance companies in Chennai city", UGC Thesis, Shodgganga.inflibnet.ac.in.

12. Gupta, D. and Gupta, M.B. (2017). "Health insurance in India-Opportunities and challenges", International Journal of Latest Technology in Engineering, Management and Applied Science, 6(1), 36-43.

13. Chauhan, V. (2019), "Medical underwriting and rating modalities in health insurance", The Journal of Inssurance Institute of India,

6(1), 14-18.

14. Devadasan, N., Ranson, K., Damme, W.V. and Criel, B. (2004). "Community health insurance in India: an overview", Health Policy, 29 (2), 133-172.

15. Dror, D.M., Radermacher, R. and Koren, R. (2006). "Willingness to pay for health insurance among rural and poor persons: Field evidence form seven micro health insurance units in India", Health Policy, 1-16.

16. Ellis, R.P., Alam, M. and Gupta, I. (2000). "Health insurance in India: Prognosis and prospectus", Economic and Political Weekly, 35 (4), 207-217.

17. Gambhir, R.S., Malhi, R., Khosla, S., Singh, R., Bhardwaj, A. and Kumar, M. (2019). "Out-patient coverage: Private sector insurance in India", Journal of Family Medicine and Primary Care, 8 (3), 788-792.

18. Gupta, D. and Gupta, M.B. (2017), "Health insurance in India-Opportunities and challenges", International Journal of Latest Technology in Engineering, Management and Applied Science, 6(1), 36-43.

19. Hand book on India Insurance Statistics re visited (2020), "Insurance regulatory and development authority website", 9-111. https://irdai.gov.in/handbook-of-indian-insurance

20. Jayaprakash, S. (2007), "An explorative study on health insurance industry in India", UGC Thesis,Shodgganga.inflibnet.ac.in.

21. Kumar, A. (2009), "Health insurance in India: is it the way forward?", World Health Statistics (WHO), 1-25.

22. Nair, S. (2019), "A comparative study of the satisfaction level of health insurance claimants of public and private sector general insurance companies", The Journal of Insurance Institute of India), 4(1), 33-42.

23. Savita (2014), "A qualitative analysis of declining membership in micro health insurance in Karma taka", SIES Journal of Management, 10 (1), 12-21.

24. Shah, A.Y.C. (2017), "Analysis of health insurance sector post liberalization in India", UGC Thesis, Shodgganga.inflibnet.ac.in.

25. Thomas, K.T. (2017), "Health insurance in India: a study on consumer insight", IRDAI Journal, 15(1), 25-31.

26. Yadav, S.C. and Sudhakar, A. (2017), "Personal factors influencing purchase decision making: a study of ealth insurance sector in India", BIMAQUEST, 17(1), 48-59.

27. Dutta, M.M. and Mitra, G. (2017), "Performance of Indian automobile insurance sector", KINDLER, 17(1), 160-168.

28. Shahi, A.K. and Gill, H.S. (2013), "Origin, growth, pattern and trends: a study of Indian health insurance sector", IOSR Journal of Humanities and Social Science, 12 (1), 1-9.

A case study on impact of Parental social status on Students' Academic Performance

✍ Manurut Tokas

Abstract

The socioeconomic status of the parents plays a significant role in determining the academic performance of their offspring. The study is an effort to determine this impact empirically. Data is collected through a structured questionnaire from two hundred students of district Bulandshahar via interviews. We have tested the impact of some socio-economic factors such as family background, father education, mother education, number of children interested in education, facilities provided by the government for children's education and decision about a child's future on the academic record of students. The findings of the study suggest that the income of father and education of both father & mother have a positive impact on the academic performance of the students. Mother education, however, has a greater impact on the academic outcomes of the students as compared to father education. Moreover, the strong family background and education facilities provided by the government also enhanced the performance of the students in the studied sample.

Keywords

Academic Performance, Government policies, Paternal socio-economic status.

Introduction

A recent wave of literature has established an important link between the socioeconomic status of a family and the learning environment available to children. It is widely believed that the social and economic status of parents can contribute significantly to student success at educational institutes. Families from the low socio-economic status group are less likely to have economic resources or time available to provide due academic support to their children. Existing literature in this field suggests that the children's initial reading capability is largely associated with the home literacy surroundings, the number of books owned and parent suffering (Barbarin & Aikens, 2015). However, parents from the low socioeconomic status groups may be powerless to meet the expense of resources such as books, computers, or tutors to produce this helpful literacy environment (Orr, 2003).

The economic status of parents, their education and reading habits are linked to each other. Moreover, parental education and reading habits have a significant influence on their kid's motivation towards learning. A study of American schoolchildren postulates that only 36% of parents from the lowest-income quintile read books daily, while the comparable figure from the highest-income quintile is 62% parents who read books every day (Cooley, 2013). Parents with higher socioeconomic status are in a better position to improve the academic activities of their children as compared to parents with low socioeconomic status(Cowen, 2011). However, some times the educational performance of these students is more questionable and controversial because the children do not follow their parent' training and do not get a good career. In addition, children with high socioeconomic status are more at risk of depletion, grade and math problems than children from low-status families (Agboola & Tsai 2012). Studies also highlight the fact that enrollment rates in schools from low-income groups are significantly lower than the children coming from families with higher socioeconomic status (Pallardi, 2008). Moreover, the dropout rates are higher for students from low-income groups as compared to the high-income families in secondary education (Center National Education Statistics, 2008). This leads us to believe that the students from poor families are less likely to complete their primary and secondary education even if they get enrolled in the schools. The social and economic status of parents, therefore, is a key factor to determine the academic performance of the students.

The academic performance and learning outcomes also determine the career opportunities available to the students in the future. It is, therefore, crucial to identify the factors affecting a student's performance. Many personal and family characteristics along with the surrounding learning and institutional environment determine these academic outcomes of the students. The study is an attempt to determine the impact of the socioeconomic status of parents on the academic record of students. We have also tried to capture the additional impact of educational facilities provided by the government on the learning outcomes of the students. We hypothesize that the socio-economic status does play a role in determining the academic performance of the students. We have conducted a survey of 200 students from the district Bulandshahar for this study. Our findings suggest that parental education, father's income, strong family background and educational facilities provided by the government have a significant impact on the academic performance of the students.

The rest of the paper is organized as follows: section two reviews relevant literature, data, and methodology are explained in section three. Findings are discussed in section four and finally study is concluded in section five of the paper.

Literature Review

The literature on the relationship between academic performance and its determinants is evolving gradually. Singh & Singh (2014) analyzed the effects of parents 'social status and family environment on students' learning habits and educational performance. Uwaifo (2008) analyzed the impact of parents' socioeconomic status on student performance in some Nigerian children and found that parents' financial status and education improved the ability of their children toward school performance. In addition, Farooq et al. (2011) analyzed the factors that affect students' quality of education. The purpose of this study was to analyze the impact of social status, parental status, and career on student achievement quality.

Ali et al. (2013) analyzed the impact of parents 'education and socioeconomic status on college students' academic performance. Kainuwa & Yusuf (2013) explained the role of socioeconomic background in the self-concept and educational success of Nigerian youth and proved the impact of students' socio-economic background on the self-conceptual and educational performance of high school students in Anamba, Nigeria. In this study, economic and social background, students' self-concept and school performance were used as variables to evaluate the school performance of students.

Balami (2015) studied the relationship between socioeconomic background and academic performance of public middle school students through a pre-learning strategy. Memon et al. (2010) analyzed the influence of parents' socioeconomic status on the performance of Karachi college students. The purpose of this study was to make recommendations based on the results of improving the educational environment. Livaditis et al. (2003) analyze students' status and academic performance and examined the impact of students' socio-economic background on school performance in Greece. Data were obtained from a sample of students enrolled in the University of Macedonia Economic and Social Studies for two consecutive academic years, 1998 and 1999.

Bolliger & Wasilik (2009) explored some factors that influence students' performance in higher education institutions. Kapinga (2014) analyzed the impact of parents' socioeconomic status on the performance of secondary education in Tanzania. The purpose of this study was to evaluate the impact of parents' socioeconomic status on the performance of high school students. Munoz et al. (1999) analyzed the impact of socioeconomic conditions on students' success in rural areas in the East.

Osorio et al. (2013)analyzed the impact of the social and educational background of Nigerian parents on the education of their children and provided parents with advice on how to overcome personal and financial challenges and how to support their children's education. Variables related to socioeconomic status, education level, and children's education were used in this study. Chandra et al. (2013) studied the impact of Lucknow's socioeconomic status on the educational outcomes of high school students and found how the different types of students' social and economic conditions affect the children's educational outcomes.

Harnish, et al. (1995) studied the development of the scale of socioeconomic background and developed a tool to assess the social and economic environment that is in line with the current situation in India. Soharwardi & Khan analyzed parental behavior in educational investment decisions and found a strong relationship between parental investment decisions and their children's education. Taras & Potts-Datema (2005) analyze the impact of socioeconomic conditions on student performance and explored the various factors that influence the outcome based on the social and economic conditions of the society.

In previous literature, the performance of students at the level of schools has been evaluated in the context of different economic, social and environmental factors. This study contributes to the existing literature in two important dimensions; (i) we have evaluated the learning outcomes of the graduation level students (ii) more emphasis has been given to the factors relating to the parents of the students.

Data and Methodology

A random sample of 200 students from the Islamia University of Bulandshahar was selected to conduct this study. The selected students were enrolled in different BS classes at the university. A structured questionnaire was developed to record the response of the selected sample. Various multiple-choice and open-ended questions were asked from the respondents. We have covered different socio-economic factors related to the students i.e. their family background, parent's education, family income, public education facilities and student' academic record in our survey. Different qualitative and quantitative methods have been employed for the analysis of this data using different tools of descriptive statistics and regression analysis.

The **Table 1** below explains the major variables used in this analysis along with the unit of measurement and codes assigned to them. The academic record of the students is used as a proxy for the academic performance of the university level students.

Table 1 Description of Variables

Variable	Measurement and Coding
Academic Record of Students(Scores)	CGPA of Students(used as dependent variable)
Social and Economic Factors for Measuring Socio-Economic Status	
Family background	0=Poor 1=Middle 2=Rich
Father Education	Years of schooling
Mother Education	Years of schooling
Father Income	Measured in rupees
Parent's Perception of their Child's Career in Future	1=Labor 2=Farmer

	3=Teacher 4=Doctor 5=Officer
Whether the student has Personal Interest in Education	Yes=1 No=0
Whether the student is satisfied with the university environment	Yes=1 No=0
Number of children	Measured in Number
Why parents want their child to obtain the education	1=For better job 2=For getting better spouses for them 3=For making them able to move in higher society
Availability of any Government education facility for the students	Yes=1 No=0

Source: Calculation from Survey

Model Specification

We have used the academic record of the students as the dependent variable measured in the cumulative grade point average (CGPA) obtained in recent examinations attended by the students. The socio-economic factors include father education, mother education, father income, family background, number of children in a family, student's satisfaction with the university environment, the parental decision about a child's future and public education facilities. Relationship between the academic performance and socio-economic status of the parents has been examined using the following linear model:

Academic Record = β_0 + β_1Family Background + β_2Father Education + β_3Mother Education + β_4Father Income + β_5Perception about Child's Career + β_6 Number of Children + β_7 Satisfaction with University + β_9 Government Facility + μ_i

Where μi is the disturbance term and academic record is the CGPA of the students obtained in the recently attempted exams. We have used the ordinary least square method for the estimation of the specified model.

Results and Discussion

Table 2 below presents the basic descriptive statistics of the variables used for empirical analysis. The table shows that 82% of the students belong to the middle class. Quite consistent with the geographic and economic conditions of district Bulandshahar where the majority of the population belongs to the middle-income group. 74.5% of the studied population reported that they are satisfied with the facilities provided by the university and the overall environment of the Islamia University of Bulandshahar, Pakistan.

Table 2 Frequency Tables of Family Background and Socioeconomic Status

Variables	Coding	Frequency	Percent	Cumulative Percent
Family Background	Poor	13	6.5	6.5
	Middle	150	75.0	81.9
	Rich	36	18.0	100.0
Students Satisfied with University Environment	No	51	25.5	25.5
	Yes	149	74.5	10
Number of Children in a Family	2	15	7.5	8.5
	3	31	15.5	24.0
	4	41	20.5	44.5
	5	47	23.5	68.0
	6	24	12.0	80.0
	7	23	11.5	91.5
	8	13	6.5	98.0

	9	4	2.0	100.0
Mother Education	0	71	35.5	35.5
	5	12	6.0	41.5
	8	12	6.0	47.5
	10	38	19.0	66.5
	11	2	1.0	67.5
	12	21	10.5	78.0
	14	27	13.5	91.5
	16	17	8.5	100.0
Perception of Parents about the Future Career of their Kid	labor	8	4.0	4.0
	farmer	23	11.5	15.5
	teacher	4	2.0	17.5
	doctor	62	31.0	48.5
	officer	103	51.5	100.0
Personal Interest of Students in Education	No	51	25.5	25.5
	Yes	149	74.5	100
Father Education	0	19	9.5	9.5
	5	3	1.5	11.0
	8	14	7.0	18.0
	10	41	20.5	38.5
	12	34	17.0	55.5
	14	41	20.5	76.0
	16	48	24.0	100.0
Father Income(in thousand rupees)	10-32	98	55	55
	34-49	48	24	24.0
	50-70	34	10	10.0
	75-100	19	8.5	8.5
	120-150	3	2.5	2.5
Availability of Government Facilities for Education	No	17	8.5	8.5
	Yes	183	91.5	100.0

Academic Record of Students	Poor	59	23.7	23.0
	Average	97	45	45.0
	Best	44	31.3	31.3

On the other hand, the students who showed dissatisfaction with the university environment were 25.5% of the population studied. The basic reason for this satisfaction was the coeducation system of the university. Since Bulandshahar district is situated in the south Punjab region of Pakistan where people at large have a conservative mindset, this dissatisfaction with the co-education system is quite consistent with the prevailing mindset in the region. Almost 64 % of families have five or more children. A higher number of children in a family may create a burden on the parents for availing better education and health facilities for their offspring. In our sample, 75% of mothers had at least primary or higher education while only 35% were illiterate.

On the other hand, the comparable figure for illiterate fathers was only 9.5% in our sample. 41% of the fathers in our sample had a bachelor's degree. As far as the perception of parents about the future career of their kids is concerned, 51% of the parents wanted their kids to become officers in the future. 31% of parents wished their children to become a doctor in future while only 4% perceived that their children will become laborers in the future. Moreover, 91.5% of parents agreed that they would send their children for higher education if the government provides different incentives and facilities for higher education. 55% of the population in our sample belongs to the income group of 10 to 32 thousand rupees per month. 79% of the studied population has income less than 50, 000 rupees per month. The academic record of the students in our sample shows that 45% of students have an average percentage of marks. 31.3% of students have a good average and 23.7% of students have a poor record of percentage in marks.

Next, we present the results obtained from the regression analysis.

Table 3 below presents the results from the ordinary least square analysis.

Table 3 Impact of Socio-Economic Factors on the Academic Performance of Students

Variables	Standardized coefficient beta	T-Stat	P-Value
Constant	1.244	9.811	0.000
Family Background	0.065	0.776	0.439
Students Satisfied with University Environment	0.046	0.666	0.506
No of Children in Family	0.093	1.3300	0.085*
Mother Education	0.346	4.307	0.000*
Perception of Parents about the Future Career of Kids	0.037	0.489	0.626
Father Education	0.146	1.745	0.083***
Father income	0.019	.219	0.087***
Availability of Government Facilities for Education	0.084	1.108	0.069*
Personal Interest of Students in Education	0.127	1.378	0.706
R-Square	0.382		
Total Observations	200		

Note: ***significant at 1%, **significant at 5%, *significant at 1%

The results of our estimation show that father and mother education has a positive and significant impact on the academic performance of the students at the university level. One year increase in father year of schooling is associated with a 14% increase in the GPA of the students.

While on the other hand, a year increase in mother education leads to a 34% increase in student's average performance. The finding shows that mother education has a stronger influence on the performance of students than the education of father.

Father income has also a positive and significant impact on the academic performance of the students. Fathers with higher incomes are found to have a higher GPA of their children. Moreover, the perception and desire of parents about their kid's future have also a positive impact on their child's performance.

The finding suggests that if parents keep higher aims for their child's career, the child is expected to put more effort into his studies and bring better grades. Similarly, the child's personal interest in education has also affected his performance positively. In addition, if the student is more concerned about his future, he is expected to bring better results. His own future career perception has a positive impact on his academic performance. Strong family background (rich family) also has a positive impact on the academic performance of the students but the coefficient is not significant in our case. According to our model results, family background has positively affected the dependent variable.

T-value is used to check the significance of the β's. The β's are significant when the value is greater than 2. The R-squared is the measure of fit of the regression equation. It gives a proportion of the variation in the dependent variable explained by the explanatory variable. Its value shows that a 33% variation in the dependent variable (academic record of the student) is due to independent variables the value of adjusted R square is .100. F statistic is used to check the overall significance of the model.

Concluding Remarks

The study is an attempt to determine the impact of the socio-economic status of parents on the academic performance of the students. Data for the analysis was collected through a structured questionnaire from 200 students. The students were selected randomly from the Islamia University of Bulandshahar, Pakistan. Various socio-economic factors such as family background, parental education, father income, perception of parents about their child's future, availability of public education facilities, etc. were accounted for the analysis. The data collected shows that the majority of the sample population belonged to the middle-income group. Regression analysis conducted in the study suggests that the parent's education affects their student's performance significantly. However, mother education is more vital for children's performance in academics. Moreover, strong family background and a father's income also impacts student performance significantly. We have also found that the parent's and students' personal perception about their bright future leads to better academic performance by the students. Public education facilities also lead to higher achievement rates of the students.

We suggest that the parents should re-examine their economic and social support to students since such support is viewed as the main contributor towards the student academic performance. The government should make public policies and plans to improve education facilities. Public policy should be oriented more towards providing cheaper, more widespread, and better educational opportunities which will lead to reduced constraints on parents' choices about sending their children to school.

References

1. Agboola, A., & Tsai, K.C. (2012). Bring character education into classroom. European Journal of Educational Research 1(2), 163-70.
2. Ali, S., Haider, Z., Munir, F., Khan, H., & Ahmed, A. (2013). Factors contributing to the students' academic performance: A case study of Islamia University Sub-Campus. American Journal of Educational Research

3. 1(8), 283-89.

4. Balami, Y.G. (2015). Relationship between self-efficacy belief and academic achievement of distance learners in National Teachers Institute (NTI) Adamawa State, Nigeria. International Journal of Education Practice

5. 3(2), 80-84.

6. Barbarin, O.A., & Aikens, N. (2015). Overcoming the educational disadvantages of poor children: How much do teacher preparation, workload, and expectations matter. American Journal of Orthopsychiatry 85(2), 101.

7. Bolliger, D.U., & Wasilik, O. (2009). Factors Influencing Faculty Satisfaction with Online Teaching and Learning in Higher Education. Distance education 30(1), 103-16.

8. Chandra, R., & Azimuddin, S. (2013). Influence of socio economic status on academic achievement of secondary school students of Lucknow city. International Journal of Scientific Engineering Research 4(12), 1952-60.

9. Cooley, A. (2013). Qualitative research in education: The origins, debates, and politics of creating knowledge. Educational Studies 49(3), 247-62.

10. Cowen, R. (2011). Edging closer to the hero, the barbarian, and the stranger: A note on the condition of comparative education. In Education systems in historical, cultural, and sociological perspectives (pp. 21-36): Brill Sense.

11. Farooq, M.S., Chaudhry, A.H., Shafiq, M., & Berhanu, G. (2011). Factors affecting students' quality of academic performance: a case of secondary school level. Journal of Quality Technology Management 7(2), 1-14.

12. Harnish, J.D., Dodge, K.A., & Valente, E. (1995). Mother-child interaction quality as a partial mediator of the roles of maternal

depressive symptomatology and socioeconomic status in the development of child behavior problems. Conduct problems prevention research group. Child development 66(3), 739-53.

13. Kainuwa, A., & Yusuf, N.B.M. (2013). Influence of socio-economic and educational background of parents on their children's education in Nigeria. International Journal of Scientific Research Publications 3(10), 1-8.

14. Kapinga, O.S. (2014). The Impact of Parental Socioeconomic Status on Students' Academic Achievement in Secondary Schools in Tanzania. International Journal of Education 6(4), 120.

15. Livaditis, M., Zaphiriadis, K., Samakouri, M., Tellidou, C., Tzavaras, N., & Xenitidis, K. (2003). Gender differences, family and psychological factors affecting school performance in Greek secondary school students. Educational Psychology, 23(2), 223-31.

16. Memon, G., Joubish, F., & Khurram, A. (2010). Impact of parental socio-economic status on students' educational achievements at secondary schools of district Malir, Karachi. Middle-East Journal of Scientific Research 6(6), 678-87.

17. Munoz, M.A., Clavijo, K.G., & Koven, S.G. (1999). Educational Equity in a Reform Environment: The Effect of Socio-Economic Status on Student Achievement.

18. Orr, A. (2003). Black-white differences in achievement: The importance of wealth. Sociology of Education 76(4), 281-304.

19. Osorio, A., Bolanc, C., Madise, N., & Rathmann, K. (2013). Social determinants of child health in Colombia: can community education moderate the effect of family characteristics? XREAP WP2.

20. Singh, A., & Singh, J.P. (2014). The influence of socio-economic status of parents and home environment on the study habits and academic achievement of students. Educational Research 5(9), 348-52.

21. Soharwardi, M.A., & Khan, A.S. Parents Behavior towards Educational Investment Decision: A Case Study of Bulandshahar, Pakistan. International Journal of Scientific & Engineering Research, 5(11), 1194-99.

22. Taras, H., & Potts-Datema, W. (2005). Chronic health conditions and student performance at school. Journal of School Health 75(7), 255-66.

23. Uwaifo, V. (2008). The effects of family structure and parenthood on the academic performance of Nigerian University students. Studies on Home Community Science, 2(2), 121-24.

Social Media and Teens: Positive & Negative Viewpoints

✍ **Saket Kumar**

Abstract

Friendship and social skills are additional areas in which the impact of social media on youth can be positive and negative. In the Pew Research Center report, 81 percent of teens in the survey said social media makes them feel more connected to what's going on in their friends' lives. In addition, two-thirds of teens said these platforms make them feel as if they have people who will support them through tough times. During the pandemic, of course, social media became one of the most frequent—and sometimes the only—way in which teens could stay connected with peers. But there's a difference between teens' social media friends vs. their real friends: The Pew survey found that 60 percent of teens say they spend time with their friends online on a daily or nearly daily basis, but only 24 percent spent time with their friends that often in person. These stats highlight how online connections may not translate into IRL relationships. In addition, the more time teens spend plugged in and on social media platforms, the more cyberbullying increases. A 2020 report by the organization L1ght found a 70 percent uptick in hate speech among kids and teens across communication channels on social media and popular chat forums. More time on social media provides enhanced access to both the beneficial and detrimental aspects, further driving the negative effects of social media on teenagers.

Keywords: social media, teens, psychological risks

Introduction

As youth mental health continues to suffer, parents, teachers, and legislators are sounding the alarm on social media. But fear and misinformation often go hand in hand. APA's recommendations aim to add science-backed balance to the discussion. "There's such a negative conversation happening around social media, and there is good reason for that. However, it's important to realize there can be benefits for many teens," said Jacqueline Nesi, PhD, an assistant professor of psychology at Brown University who studies technology use in youth, and a member of the APA panel that produced the health advisory. "Teens (and adults) obviously get something out of social media. We have to take a balanced view if we want to reach teens and help them use these platforms in healthier ways."

In 2023, an estimated 4.9 billion people worldwide are expected to use social media. For teens who grew up with technology, those digital platforms are woven into the fabric of their lives. "Social media is here to stay," said Mary Alvord, PhD, a clinical psychologist in Maryland and adjunct professor at George Washington University, and a member of the APA panel. That doesn't mean we have to accept its dangers, however. "Just as we decide when kids are old enough to drive, and we teach them to be good drivers, we can establish guidelines and teach children to use social media safely," Alvord said.

Social media charms and harms

Even before the COVID-19 pandemic, rates of depression, anxiety, and suicide in young people were climbing. In 2021, more than 40% of high school students reported depressive symptoms, with girls and LGBTQ+ youth reporting even higher rates of poor mental health and suicidal thoughts, according to data from the U.S. Centers for Disease Control and Prevention (American Economic Review, Vol. 112, No. 11, 2022).

Young people may be particularly vulnerable to social media's charms—as well as its harms. During adolescent development, brain regions associated with the desire for attention, feedback, and reinforcement from peers become more sensitive. Meanwhile, the brain regions involved in self-control have not fully matured. That can be a recipe for disaster. "The need to prioritize peers is a normal part of adolescent development, and youth are turning to social media for some of that longed-for peer contact," said clinical psychologist Mary Ann McCabe, PhD, ABPP, a member-at-large of APA's Board of Directors, adjunct associate professor of pediatrics at George Washington University School of Medicine, and cochair of the expert advisory panel. "The original yearning is social, but kids can accidentally wander into harmful content."

The potential risks of social media may be especially acute during early adolescence when puberty delivers an onslaught of biological, psychological, and social changes. One longitudinal analysis of data from youth in the United Kingdom found distinct developmental windows during which adolescents are especially sensitive to social media's impact. During those windows—around 11 to 13 for girls and 14 to 15 for boys—more social media use predicts a decrease in life satisfaction a year later, while lower use predicts greater life satisfaction (Orben, A., et al., Nature Communications, Vol. 13, No. 1649, 2022).

One takeaway from such research is that adults should monitor kids' social media use closely in early adolescence, between the ages of 10 and 14 or so. As kids become more mature and develop digital literacy skills, they can earn more autonomy.

The cost of connection

The internet is at its best when it brings people together. Adults can help kids get the most out of social media by encouraging them to use online platforms to engage with others in positive ways. "The primary benefit is social connection, and that's true for teens who are connecting with friends they already have or making new connections," Nesi said. "On social media, they can find people who share their identities and interests."

Online social interaction can promote healthy socialization among teens, especially when they're experiencing stress or social isolation. For youth who have anxiety or struggle in social situations, practicing conversations over social media can be an important step toward feeling more comfortable interacting with peers in person. Social media can also help kids stay in touch with their support networks. That can be especially important for kids from marginalized groups, such as LGBTQ+ adolescents who may be reluctant or unable to discuss their identity with caregivers (Craig, S. L., et al., Social Media + Society, Vol. 7, No. 1, 2021). In such cases, online support can be a lifeline. "We know from suicide prevention research that it's critical for people to know they aren't alone," Alvord said.

Kids also learn about themselves online. "Social media provides a lot of opportunities for young people to discover new information, learn about current events, engage with issues, and have their voices heard," Nesi added. "And it gives them an opportunity to explore their identities, which is an important task of the adolescent years."

Yet all those opportunities come at a cost. "There is a lot of good that can come from social media. The problem is, the algorithms can also lead you down rabbit holes," Alvord said. Technology is expertly designed to pull us in. Features such as "like" buttons, notifications, and videos that start playing automatically make it incredibly hard to step away. At the extreme, social media use can interfere with sleep, physical activity, schoolwork, and in-person social interactions. "The risk of technologies that pull us in is that they can get in the way of all the things we know are important for a teen's development," Nesi said.

Research suggests that setting limits and boundaries around social media, combined with discussion and coaching from adults, is the best way to promote positive outcomes for youth (Wachs, S., et al., Computers & Education, Vol. 160, No. 1, 2021). Parents should talk to kids often about social media and technology and also use strategies like limiting the amount of time kids can use devices and removing devices from the bedroom at night. Caregivers should also keep an eye out for problematic behaviors, such as strong cravings to use social media, an inability to stop, and lying or sneaking around in order to use devices when they aren't allowed.

In helping to set boundaries around social media, it's important that parents don't simply limit access to devices, Alvord added. "Removing devices can feel punitive. Instead, parents should focus on encouraging kids to spend time with other activities they find valuable, such as movement and art activities they enjoy," she said. "When kids are spending more time on those things, they're less likely to be stuck on social media."

Dangerous content

Spending too much time on social media is one cause for concern. Dangerous content is another. Despite efforts by caregivers and tech companies to protect kids from problematic material, they still encounter plenty of it online—including mis- and disinformation, racism and hate speech, and content that promotes dangerous behaviors such as disordered eating and self-harm.

During the first year of the pandemic, when kids were spending more time at home and online, McCabe saw a flurry of new diagnoses of eating disorders in her teen patients and their friends. "These kids often reported that they started by watching something relatively benign, like exercise videos," she said. But their social media algorithms doubled down on that content, offering up more and more material related to body image and weight. "It was an echo chamber," McCabe added. "And several of my patients attributed their eating disorders to this online behavior."

Unfortunately, McCabe's observations seem to be part of a common pattern. A large body of research, cited in APA's health advisory, suggests that using social media for comparisons and feedback related to physical appearance is linked to poorer body image, disordered eating, and depressive symptoms, especially among girls.

Other research shows that when youth are exposed to unsafe behaviors online, such as substance use or self-harm, they may be at greater risk of engaging in similar behaviors themselves. In a longitudinal study of high school students, Nesi and colleagues showed that kids who saw their peers drinking alcohol on social media were more likely to start drinking and to binge drink 1 year later, even after controlling for demographic and developmental risk factors (Journal of Adolescent Health, Vol. 60, No. 6, 2017).

Cyberbullying is another source of worry, both for young people and their caregivers. Indeed, research shows that online bullying and harassment can be harmful for a young person's psychological well-being. APA's health advisory cited several studies that found online bullying and harassment can be more severe than offline bullying. The research showed it can increase the risk of mental health problems in adolescents—with risks for both perpetrators and victims of cyberhate.

Ingrained racism

Search engines and social media algorithms can expose adolescents to other types of cyberhate, including racism. In fact, online algorithms often have structural racism and bias baked in, in ways that White users might not even notice. Sometimes, the algorithms themselves churn out biased or racist content. TikTok, for instance, has come under fire for recommending new accounts based on the appearance of the people a user already follows—with the inadvertent effect of segregating the platform. In addition to this form of "algorithmic bias," people of color are frequently subjected to what some researchers call "filter bias." In one common example, the beauty filters built into sites like Instagram or Snapchat might apply paler skin or more typically White facial features to a user's selfies.

Like microaggressions in offline life, online racism in the form of algorithmic and filter bias can take a toll on mental health, said Brendesha Tynes, PhD, a professor of education and psychology at the University of Southern California, and a member of the APA advisory panel. In an ongoing daily diary study with adolescents, she is finding evidence that people who are exposed to algorithmic and filter bias are at increased risk of next-day depression and anxiety symptoms.

"I'm an adult who studies these issues and who has a lot of strategies to protect myself, and it can still be really hard" to cope with online racism, she said. Impressionable teens who haven't learned such strategies are likely to experience even greater psychological impacts from the racism they encounter every day on social media. "We're just beginning to understand the profound negative impacts of online racism," Tynes said. "We need all hands on deck in supporting kids of color and helping them cope with these experiences."

Despite the drawbacks of technology, there is a silver lining. Tynes has found Black youth receive valuable social support from other Black people on social media. Those interactions can help them learn to think critically about the racism they encounter. That's important, since her research also shows that youth who are able to critique racism experience less psychological distress when they witness race-related traumatic events online (Journal of Adolescent Health, Vol. 43, No. 6, 2008).

Tynes said more research is needed to understand how online racism affects youth and how best to protect them from its harms.

"Different groups have vastly different experiences online," she said. "We need more detailed recommendations for specific groups."

A role for psychology

How to protect kids from online racism is just one of a long list of questions on researchers' wish lists. Digital technologies evolve so quickly that kids are off to a new platform before scientists can finish collecting data about yesterday's favorite sites. "There's so much we still don't know about this topic. That's understandably frustrating for people because social media is impacting people's lives as we speak," Nesi said.

It's likely some groups, and some individuals, are more susceptible than others to the negative effects of social media, she added. "We need more information about who is more vulnerable and who is more resilient, and what it is they're doing online that's healthy versus harmful."

While there is a lot of work to be done, Nesi said, "we're getting closer." As APA's recommendations make clear, there is ample evidence some types of content and online behaviors can harm youth. Adult role models can work together with teens to understand the pitfalls of technology and establish boundaries to protect them from dangerous content and excessive screen time. Psychological research shows children from a young age should be taught digital literacy skills such as identifying misinformation, protecting privacy, understanding how people can misrepresent themselves online, and how to critically evaluate race-related materials online. One way to promote those skills may be to lean into teens' inherent skepticism of grown-ups. "You can teach kids that a lot of people want something from them," Alvord said—whether it's a stranger trying to message them on Instagram, or TikTok earning money by collecting their data or showing them branded content.

That's not to say it's easy to help kids develop a healthy relationship with social media. "By necessity, adolescents disagree more with their parents—and they are formidable when they insist on having something, like phones or social media, that all their friends have," McCabe said. "But parents are eager for guidance. There is an appetite for this information now," she added—and psychological scientists can help provide it.

That scientific research can inform broader efforts to keep children safe on social media as well. "Parents can't do this alone," Nesi said. "We need larger-scale changes to these platforms to protect kids."

There are efforts to make such changes. The Kids Online Safety Act, a bipartisan bill introduced in April, establishes a duty of care for social media companies to protect minors from mental health harms, sex trafficking, narcotics, and other dangers. Additionally, the bill requires social media companies to go through independent, external audits, allows researcher access to platform data assets, and creates substantial youth and parental controls to create a safer digital environment. Even as legislators and tech companies consider those and other policies, researchers can continue their efforts to determine which actions might be most protective, said Nesi, who is currently leading a study to understand which features of social media are helpful versus harmful for kids at high risk of suicide. "For some kids, being able to connect with others and find support is really important. For others, social media may create more challenges than it solves," Nesi said. "The key is making sure we don't accidentally do any harm" by enacting restrictions and legislation that are not backed by science.

While researchers forge ahead, clinical psychologists, too, can add valuable insight for teens and their families. "Screens are a central part of adolescents' lives, and that needs to be integrated into assessment and treatment," Nesi said. "Clinicians can help families and teens take a step back and look at their social media use to figure out what's working for them and what isn't."

Someday, McCabe said, digital literacy may be taught in schools the same way that youth learn about sexual health and substance use. "I hope we'll come to a point where teaching about the healthy use of social media is an everyday occurrence," she said. "Because of this dialogue that we're having now among families and policymakers, we may see a new generation of kids whose entry into the digital world is very different, where we can use social media for connection and education but minimize the harms," she added. "I hope this is the beginning of a new day."

Conclusion

Friendship and social skills are additional areas in which the impact of social media on youth can be positive and negative. In the Pew Research Center report, 81 percent of teens in the survey said social media makes them feel more connected to what's going on in their friends' lives. In addition, two-thirds of teens said these platforms make them feel as if they have people who will support them through tough times.

During the pandemic, of course, social media became one of the most frequent—and sometimes the only—way in which teens could stay connected with peers. But there's a difference between teens' social media friends vs. their real friends: The Pew survey found that 60 percent of teens say they spend time with their friends online on a daily or nearly daily basis, but only 24 percent spent time with their friends that often in person. These stats highlight how online connections may not translate into IRL relationships. In addition, the more time teens spend plugged in and on social media platforms, the more cyberbullying increases. A 2020 report by the organization L1ght found a 70 percent uptick in hate speech among kids and teens across communication channels on social media and popular chat forums. More time on social media provides enhanced access to both the beneficial and detrimental aspects, further driving the negative effects of social media on teenagers.

References

1. Algorithms of oppression: How search engines reinforce racism Noble, S. U., New York University Press, 2018
2. Family Online Safety Institute: An updated agenda for the study of

digital media use and adolescent development: Future directions following Odgers & Jensen (2020)

3. Prinstein, M. J., et al., The Journal of Child Psychology and Psychiatry, 2020: From Google searches to Russian disinformation: Adolescent critical race digital literacy needs and skills

4. Tynes, B., et al., International Journal of Multicultural Education, 2021

5. How social media affects teen mental health: A missing link: Orben, A., & Blakemore, S.J. Nature, Feb. 14, 2023

Service Marketing: A Review

✍ **Prarthna Singh**

Abstract

Marketing literature has taken a giant leap from goods logic to service dominant logic. From beginning, marketing has been expanding its horizons to include exchanges except goods. Services being processual in nature impacts consumer behaviour differently from that of goods. Marketing for tangibles revolves around the tangible product whereas in case of service marketing, consumers are integral part of whole process.The uncertainty level in service purchase is higher and therefore marketers need to provide adequate information to satisfy the informational needs of consumers. The consumer contact employees should be trained well. Building relationships are key factors in marketing of services. Risk is perceived to be higher in case of services. In case of goods, it is easier to be certain about the proposed purchase. But in case of services, the consumer cannot know with certainty about the service offering before purchase. Experience with the first purchase is very important in case of services. The marketers should offer incentives to consumers to try out their service. It has been established in literature that personal sources are more credible and preferred source of information in case of services. Thus, marketers should focus on increasing user generated content by encouraging review, ratings and recommendations by consumers. Referral marketing is very effective in case of services.

Internet has been enormous facilitator in marketing of services. Social media marketing especially user generated content has become a key element in service promotion mix. Indeed, service marketing is full of challenges and opportunities. Service marketing as a field of study has not yet reached maturity. Future studies on service marketing can explore dimensions such as service experience co-creation, digital service space and role of e-WOM in service marketing.

Keywords: Services, Marketing Mix, Marketing

Introduction

A traditional definition of marketing is provided by the Chartered Institute of Marketing: The management process which identifies anticipates and supplies customer requirements efficiently and profitably. (Palmer, 2004, P.8)

The marketing mix for services:

The marketing mix for services is not only the same as by the Goods marketers. They have the 4Ps: Product Place Promotion Price. Early analysis by Borden (1965) of marketing mix elements was based on a study of manufacturing industry at a time when the importance of services to the economy was considered to be relatively unimportant. More recently, the 4Ps of the marketing mix have been found to be too limited in their application to services. Particular problems that limit their usefulness to services are as follows. (Palmer, 2004 P.10)

4Ps:

Product:

Products are something which is produced by physical act or labor. In marketing, a product is anything that can be offered to a market that might satisfy a want or need. However, it is much more than just a physical object. It is the complete bundle of benefits or satisfactions that buyers perceive they will obtain if they purchase the product. It is the sum of all physical, psychological, symbolic, and service attributes.

Pricing:

Pricing is one of the four aspects of marketing. The other three parts of the marketing mix are product management, promotion, and distribution. It is also a key variable in microeconomic price allocation theory. Pricing is the manual or automatic process of applying prices to purchase and sales orders, based on factors such as: a fixed amount, quantity break, promotion or sales campaign, specific vendor quote, price prevailing on entry, shipment or invoice date, combination of multiple orders or lines, and many others. Automated systems require more setup and maintenance but may prevent pricing errors.

Promotion:

The specification of these four variables creates a promotional mix or promotional plan. A promotional mix specifies how much attention to pay to each of the four subcategories, and how much money to budget for each. A promotional plan can have a wide range of objectives, including: sales increases, new product acceptance, creation of brand equity, positioning, competitive retaliations, or creation of a corporate image

+2 or 3 Ps:

In the context of services marketing, Booms and Bitner (1981) have therefore suggested an extended "7-Ps" approach that contains the following additional "Ps":

People:

All people directly or indirectly involved in the consumption of a service, e.g. employees or other consumers. An essential ingredient to any service provision is the use of appropriate staff and people. Recruiting the right staff and training them appropriately in the delivery of their service is essential if the organization wants to obtain a form of competitive advantage. Consumers make judgements and deliver perceptions of the service based on the employees they interact with. Staff should have the appropriate interpersonal skills, attitude, and service knowledge to provide the service that consumers are paying for. Many British organizations aim to apply for the Investors In People accreditation, which tells consumers that staff are taken care off by the company and they are trained to certain standards (www.learnmarketing.net/servicemarketingmix.htm)

Process:

Procedure, mechanisms and flow of activities by which services are consumed. The additional "P" of "processes": "How" a product is produced becomes increasingly crucial to a large number of consumers – just think about cosmetics (animal testing) or cars (recycling).

The biggest advantage of this discussion however is probably that those who discuss it deepen their own knowledge – not only about the marketing mix in particular but also about marketing in general.

Physical Evidence:

The environment in which the service is delivered. It also includes tangible goods that help to communicate and perform the service. The first two additional Ps are explicit (People, Process) and the third one (Physical Evidence) is an implicit factor. Where is the service being delivered? Physical Evidence is the element of the service mix which allows the consumer again to make judgements on the organization. If you walk into a restaurant your expectations are of a clean, friendly environment. On an aircraft if you travel first class you expect enough room to be able to lay down!

"Managing the evidence" refers to the act of informing customers that the service encounter has been performed successfully. It is best done in subtle ways like providing examples or descriptions of good and poor service that can be used as a basis of comparison. The underlying rationale is that a customer might not appreciate the full worth of the service if they do not have a good benchmark for comparisons. (Levitt)

The dichotomy between physical goods and intangible services should not be given too much credence. These are not discrete categories. Most business theorists see a continuum with pure service on one terminal point and pure commodity good on the other terminal point. Most products fall between these two extremes. For example, a restaurant provides a physical good (the food), but also provides services in the form of ambience, the setting and clearing of the table, etc. And although some utilities actually deliver physical goods — like water utilities which actually deliver water — utilities are usually treated as services.

The service-goods continuum

Distinguishing features of services

Zeithaml, Parasuraman, and Berry sum up four common factors that characterize all services: intangibility, inseparability of production and consumption, perishability, and heterogeneity. Services are said to be **intangible** because they are performances rather than objects, and they cannot be touched or seen in the same manner as goods; rather, they are experienced, and consumers' judgments about hem tend to be more subjective than objective. (Bateson, 1995. P9)

Inseparability:

Services cannot be separated from the service providers. A product when produced can be taken away from the producer. However, a service is produced at or near the point of purchase. Take visiting a restaurant, you order your meal, the waiting and delivery of the meal, the service provided by the waiter/rests is all a part of the service production process and is inseparable, the staff in a restaurant are as apart of the process as well as the quality of food provided.

(http://users.wbs.warwick.ac.uk/dibb_simkin/student/glossary/ch11.ht ml)

Perishability:

Services last a specific time and cannot be stored like a product for later use. If travelling by train, coach or air the service will only last the duration of the journey. The service is developed and used almost simultaneously.

Again because of this time constraint consumers demand more. A characteristic of services whereby unused capacity on one occasion cannot be stockpiled or inventoried for future occasions. (Dibb Simkin Pride Ferrel P. 324)

Heterogeneity:

Heterogeneity refers to the potential for variability in the performance of services and problems of lack of consistency that cannot be eliminated in services as they frequently can be with goods.(Baeteson P11.)

It is very difficult to make each service experience identical. If travelling by plane the service quality may differ from the first time you travelled by that airline to the second, because the airhostess is more or less experienced. A concert performed by a group on two nights may differ in slight ways because it is very difficult to standardize every dance move. Generally systems and procedures are put into place to make sure the service provided is consistent all the time, training in service organizations is essential for this, however in saying this there will always be subtle differences.

Conclusion

Marketing literature has taken a giant leap from goods logic to service dominant logic. From beginning, marketing has been expanding its horizons to include exchanges except goods. Services being processual in nature impacts consumer behavior differently from that of goods. Marketing for tangibles revolves around the tangible product whereas in case of service marketing, consumers are integral part of whole process. The uncertainty level in service purchase is higher and therefore marketers need to provide adequate information to satisfy the informational needs of consumers. The consumer contact employees should be trained well. Building relationships are key factors in marketing of services. Risk is perceived to be higher in case of services. In case of goods, it is easier to be certain about the proposed purchase. But in case of services, the consumer cannot know with certainty about the service offering before purchase. Experience with the first purchase is very important in case of services.

References:

1. Palmer, Adrian: Principles of Services Marketing 4th edition 2005
2. Levitt, T. (1981) "Managing intangible products and product intangibles", Harvard Business Review, May-June, 1981, pp.94-102
3. Booms, B. H. and Mary-Joe Bitner (1981), "Marketing Strategies and Organization Structures for Service Firms", in Marketing of Services, J. H. Donnelly and W. R. George, Eds. Chicago: American Marketing Association.
4. K. Douglas Hoffman John E.G. Baeteson Essential of Service Marketing 1997.
5. John E.G. Baeteson Managing Services Marketing Text and Readings 3rd edition 1995.
6. Dibb Simkin Pride Ferrel, Marketing 4th Edition Houghton Mifflin by the Warwick University, England.
7. www.learnmarketing.net/servicemarketingmix.html.
8. Donald Cowell the Marketing of Services 1993, Oxford

A Review on New Media Role in politics

✍ Shailendra Kumar

Introduction

New political media are forms of communication that facilitate the production, dissemination, and exchange of political content on platforms and within networks that accommodate interaction and collaboration. They have evolved rapidly over the past three decades, and continue to develop in novel, sometimes unanticipated ways. New media have wide-ranging implications for democratic governance and political practices. They have radically altered the ways in which government institutions operate and political leaders communicate. They have transformed the political media system, and redefined the role of journalists. They have redefined the way elections are contested, and how citizens engage in politics.

The rise of new media has complicated the political media system. Legacy media consisting of established mass media institutions that predate the Internet, such as newspapers, radio shows, and television news programs, coexist with new media that are the outgrowth of technological innovation. While legacy media maintain relatively stable formats, the litany of new media, which includes websites, blogs, video-sharing platforms, digital apps, and social media, are continually expanding in innovative ways. Mass media designed to deliver general interest news to broad audiences have been joined by niche sources that narrowcast to discrete users (Stroud, 2011). New media can relay information directly to individuals without the intervention of editorial or institutional gatekeepers, which are intrinsic to legacy forms. Thus, new media have introduced an increased level of instability and unpredictability into the political communication process.

The relationship between legacy media and new media is symbiotic. Legacy media have incorporated new media into their reporting strategies. They distribute material across an array of old and new communication platforms. They rely on new media sources to meet the ever-increasing demand for content. Despite competition from new media, the audiences for traditional media remain robust, even if they are not as formidable as in the past. Readers of the print edition of The New York Times and viewers of the nightly network news programs far outnumber those accessing the most popular political news websites (Wired Staff, 2017). Cable and network television news remain the primary sources of political information for people over the age of thirty (Mitchell and Holcomb, 2016). Consequently, new media rely on their legacy counterparts to gain legitimacy and popularize their content.

Ideally, the media serve several essential roles in a democratic society. Their primary purpose is to inform the public, providing citizens with the information needed to make thoughtful decisions about leadership and policy. The media act as watchdogs checking government actions. They set the agenda for public discussion of issues, and provide a forum for political expression. They also facilitate community building by helping people to find common causes, identify civic groups, and work toward solutions to societal problems.

New media have the potential to satisfy these textbook functions. They provide unprecedented access to information, and can reach even disinterested audience members through personalized, peer-to-peer channels, like Facebook. As average people join forces with the established press to perform the watchdog role, public officials are subject to greater scrutiny. Issues and events that might be outside the purview of mainstream journalists can be brought into prominence by ordinary citizens. New media can foster community building that transcends physical boundaries through their extensive networking capabilities. Although legacy media coverage of political events correlates with increased political engagement among the mass public, mainstream journalists do not believe that encouraging participation is their responsibility (Hayes and Lawless, 2016). However, new media explicitly seek to directly engage the public in political activities, such as voting, contacting public officials, volunteering in their communities, and taking part in protest movements.

At the same time, the new media era has acerbated trends that undercut the ideal aims of a democratic press. The media disseminate a tremendous amount of political content, but much of the material is trivial, unreliable, and polarizing. The watchdog role pre-new media had been performed largely by trained journalists who, under the best of circumstances, focused on uncovering the facts surrounding serious political transgressions. Washington Post reporters Bob Woodward and Carl Bernstein inspired a generation of investigative journalists after revealing President Richard Nixon's role in the break-in at the Democratic Party headquarters at the Watergate Hotel, forcing his resignation (Shepard, 2012). Much news in the new media era is defined by coverage of a never-ending barrage of sensational scandals—be they real, exaggerated, or entirely fabricated—that often are only tangentially related to governing.

This chapter begins by briefly addressing the evolution of new media in the United States to establish the core characteristics of the current political media system. We then will focus on the role of media in providing information in a democratic polity, and will examine the ways in which new media have impacted this role. The diversity of content disseminated by new media has created opportunities, such as the ability for more voices to be heard. However, the questionable quality of much of this information raises serious issues for democratic discourse. Next, we will discuss how the new media are integral to political coverage in a post-truth society, where falsehoods infused with tidbits of fact pass as news. Finally, we will contemplate the ways in which the watchdog press is being overshadowed by the mouthpiece press which serves as a publicity machine for politicians.

THE EVOLUTION OF NEW MEDIA

New media emerged in the late 1980s when entertainment platforms, like talk radio, television talk shows, and tabloid newspapers, took on prominent political roles and gave rise to the infotainment genre. Infotainment obscures the lines between news and entertainment, and privileges sensational, scandal-driven stories over hard news (Jebril, et al., 2013). Politicians turned to new media to circumvent the mainstream press' control over the news agenda. The infotainment emphasis of new media at this early stage offered political leaders and candidates a friendlier venue for presenting themselves to the public than did hard news outlets (Moy, et al., 2009). During the 1992 presidential election, Democratic candidate Bill Clinton famously appeared on Arsenio Hall's television talk show wearing sunglasses and playing the saxophone, which created a warm, personal image that set the tone for his campaign (Diamond, et al., 1993). The fusing of politics and entertainment attracted audiences that typically had been disinterested in public affairs (Williams and Delli Carpini, 2011). It also prompted the ascendance of celebrity politicians, and set the stage for a "reality TV" president like Donald Trump decades later.

Political observers and scholars contemplated the advent of a "new media populism" that would engage disenfranchised citizens and facilitate a more active role for the public in political discourse. New media had the potential to enhance people's access to political information, facilitate wider-ranging political discourse, and foster participation. Initially, the public responded positively to the more accessible communication channels, calling in to political talk programs and participating in online town hall meetings. However, new media's authentic populist potential was undercut by the fact that the new political media system evolved haphazardly, with no guiding principles or goals. It was heavily dominated by commercial interests and those already holding privileged positions in politics and the news industry. Public enthusiasm eventually gave way to ambivalence and cynicism, especially as the novelty of the first phase of new media wore off (Davis and Owen, 1998).

The next phase in the development of new media unfolded in conjunction with the application of emerging digital communications technologies to politics that made possible entirely new outlets and content delivery systems. The digital environment and the platforms it supports greatly transformed the political media system. Beginning in the mid-1990s, new political media platforms quickly progressed from the rudimentary "brochureware" website, used by Bill Clinton's presidential campaign in 1992, to encompass sites with interactive features, discussion boards, blogs, online fundraising platforms, volunteer recruitment sites, and meet-ups. The public became more involved with the actual production and distribution of political content. Citizen journalists were eyewitnesses to events that professional journalists did not cover. Non-elites offered their perspectives on political affairs to politicians and peers. Members of the public also were responsible for recording and posting videos that could go viral and influence the course of events (Wallsten, 2010). In 2006, for example, the reelection campaign of Republican Senator George Allen was derailed by a viral video in which he used the term "macaca," a racial slur, to refer to a young man of Indian ancestry who was attending his campaign rally (Craig and Shear, 2006).

A third phase in the evolution of new media is marked by Democratic candidate Barack Obama's groundbreaking digital campaign strategy in the 2008 presidential election. Obama's team revolutionized the use of social media in an election they felt was unwinnable using traditional techniques. The campaign made use of advanced digital media features that capitalized on the networking, collaboration, and community-building potential of social media to create a political movement. The Obama campaign website was a full-service, multimedia center where voters not only could access information, they also could watch and share videos, view and distribute campaign ads, post comments, and blog. Supporters could donate, volunteer, and purchase campaign logo items, like tee shirts and caps. The campaign was active on Facebook, Twitter, and YouTube, as well as a range of other social media platforms that catered to particular constituencies, such as BlackPlanet, AsianAve, and Glee. The campaign pioneered digital microtargeting tactics. It used social media to collect data on people's political and consumer preferences, and created voter profiles to pursue specific groups, such as young professional voters, with customized messages.

The new media trends established in the 2008 campaign have carried over to the realm of government and politics more generally. Social media have become a pervasive force in politics, altering the communication dynamics between political leaders, journalists, and the public. They have opened up wider avenues for instantaneous political discourse and debate. Research indicates that people's access to social media networks has a positive effect on their sense of political efficacy and tendency to participate in politics (Gil de Zuniga, et al., 2010). However, there also has been backlash when social media discourse has become too nasty, and users have blocked content or dropped out of their social media networks (Linder, 2016). Social media allow people to efficiently organize and leverage their collective influence. Thus, political leaders are held more accountable because their actions are constantly probed on social media.

At the same time, legacy media organizations have come to rely on aspects of new media. Newspapers, in particular, have experienced financial hardships due adverse financial market conditions, declining advertising revenues, and competition from proliferating news sources. The size of traditional newsrooms in the U.S. has shrunk by more than 20,000 positions in the past twenty years, and global newsrooms have experienced a similar decline (Owen, 2017). Legacy news organizations have cut investigative units, and only around one-third of reporters are assigned to political beats (Mitchell and Holcomb, 2016). Alicia Shepard, a former media ombudsman and media literacy advocate, opined, "When newspapers can't even cover daily journalism, how are they going to invest in long-term, expensive investigative reporting?" (2012). Still, journalists working for legacy organizations continue to do the yeoman's share of serious news gathering and investigative reporting. Mainstream journalists have come to rely heavily on new media content as a source of news. These trends have seriously influenced the quality and nature of news content as well as the style of political reporting, which has become more heavily infused with infotainment and quotes from Twitter feeds.

PROVIDING POLITICAL INFORMATION

The complexities of the new media system are reflected in the diversity of available content. The information distributed via the vast communications network runs the gamut from fact-based, investigative reporting from professional journalists to brash fabrications or "alternative facts"—to use the term coined by President Trump's advisor Kellyanne Conway—proffered by the alternative press (Graham, 2017). In the new media era, the boundaries that separate these disparate types of information have become increasing muddled. Professional media editors who regulate the flow of information by applying news principles and standards associated with the public good have become scarce (Willis,

1987). They have been replaced by social media and analytics editors whose primary motivation is to draw users to content regardless of its news value. Audience members have to work hard to distinguish fact from fiction, and to differentiate what matters from what is inconsequential.

A number of explanations can be offered for the shift in the quality and quantity of political information. The technological affordances of new media allow content to propagate seemingly without limits. Social media have a dramatically different structure than previous media platforms. Content can be relayed with no significant third-party filtering, fact-checking, or editorial judgement. Individuals lacking prior journalism training or reputation can reach many users at lightningfast speed. Messages multiply as they are shared across news platforms and via personal social networking accounts (Allcott and Gentzkow, 2017).

In addition, the economic incentives underpinning new media companies, such as Google, Facebook, and Twitter, are predicated on attracting large audiences that will draw advertising revenue. Political content is used to drive consumers to social media products, rather than to perform the public service function of informing the citizenry. Commercial pressures lead media organizations to feature incendiary stories that receive the most attention. Further, while platforms proliferate, similar content is dispersed widely as media power is concentrated in a small number of old and new media corporations (McChesney, 2015). Search engines direct users to a limited selection of heavily trafficked and well-financed sites (Hindman, 2009; Pariser, 2011).

Other explanations focus on the nature of the American political environment that has become extremely polarized, prompting the emergence of political agendas that promote rogue politics. A 2017 Pew Research Center study revealed that the gap between Democrats and Republicans on core political values, including the role of government, race, immigration, the social safety net, national security, taxes, and environmental protection, have grown to epic proportions for the modern era. Two-thirds of Americans fall solidly in the liberal or conservative camp, with few holding a mix of ideological positions (Pew Research Center, 2017; Kiley, 2017).

Speech on new media reflects these stark political divisions, and frequently devolves into expressions of hostility and ad hominem attacks. President Donald Trump used Twitter to ignite a controversy over NFL players who protested racial oppression during the playing of the national anthem before games. He used a derogatory term to refer to players, who are predominantly African American, and urged team owners to fire those supporting the demonstration. Trump's social media blasts accused the players of disrespecting the flag and the military, which misrepresents the protest agenda and has divided the public along political and racial lines.

Political divisions are reflected in the presence of media "echo chambers," where people select their news and information sources based on their affinity for the politics of other users. Modern-day new media echo chambers began to form during the first phase of new media, as conservative talk radio hosts, like Rush Limbaugh, attracted dedicated followers (Jamieson and Cappella, 2010). Social media has hastened the development of echo chambers, as they facilitate people's exposure to information shared by like-minded individuals in their personal digital networks, with 62% of adult Americans getting their news from social media platforms. Even politically disinterested social media users frequently encounter news articles unintentionally as they scan their feed (Gottfried and Shearer, 2016). The ability of social media to isolate people from exposure to those with differing viewpoints exacerbates political polarization.

A significant segment of the public perceives journalists as removed elites who do not share their conservative values. Political analyst Nate Silver (2017) contends that the national press has been operating in a politically homogenous, metropolitan, liberal-leaning bubble that has become attached to "Establishment Influentials". He maintains that the mainstream media are out-of-touch with a wide swath of the public. During the recent election this became clear as legacy media institutions are unable to connect effectively with the frustration and anger of people outside of high education and income circles (Camosy, 2016).

Some scholars argue that new media are closing the gap between distant journalists and the mass public by giving voice to those who have felt left out (Duggan and Smith, 2016). The Tea Party, a conservative political movement focused around issues about taxation and the national debt, used social networks for political mobilization in the 2010 midterm elections. Tea Party candidates employed social media to reshape public discourse around the campaign, forging a sense of solidarity among groups who previously felt disenfranchised (Williamson, Skocpol, and Coggin, 2011). Candidates pushing an extreme agenda have amplified this trend. Highly partisan, flamboyant congressional candidates, on both sides of the aisle, who spark political disagreement and indignant rhetoric garner the most supporters on Facebook. They use social media to solidify their political base (Messing and Weisel, 2017).

POST-TRUTH MEDIA

American author Ralph Keyes (2004) observes that society has entered a posttruth era. Deception has become a defining characteristic of modern life, and is so pervasive that people are desensitized to its implications. He laments the fact that ambiguous statements containing a kernel of authenticity, but falling short of the truth, have become the currency of politicians, reporters, corporate executives, and other power-brokers.

Journalist Susan Glasser (2016) argues that journalism has come to reflect the realities of reporting in post-truth America. Objective facts are subordinate to emotional appeals and personal beliefs in shaping public opinion. The public has difficulty distinguishing relevant news about weighty policy issues from the extraneous clamor that permeates the media. The work of investigative journalists has in some ways has become more insightful and informed than in the past due to the vast resources available for researching stories, including greater access to government archives and big data analysis. However, well-documented stories are obscured by the constant drone of repetitive, sensationalized trivia-bites that dominate old and new media. Reflecting on coverage of the last American presidential contest, Glasser states, "The media scandal of 2016 isn't so much about what reporters fail to tell the American public; it's about what they did report on, and the fact that it didn't seem to matter" (2016).

Evidence that Glasser's concerns are well-founded can be compiled by examining media content on a daily basis. Post-truth media was prominent during the 2016 presidential election. Media accounts of the election were infused with misinformation, baseless rumors, and outright lies. False stories and unverified factoids emanated from fabricated news sites as well as the social media accounts of the candidates and their surrogates. Republican nominee Donald Trump used his Twitter feed to push out sensational, unverified statements that would dominate the news agenda, a practice he maintained after assuming the presidency. He alleged that the father of Ted Cruz, his challenger for the nomination, was involved in the assassination of President John F. Kennedy, and perpetuated the false claim that President Barack Obama was not born in the United States (Carson, 2017). False news stories infiltrated reports by legacy media organizations as they relied heavily on digital sources for information. Cable news organizations like CNN and MSNBC amplified Trump's unfounded claims, such as his allegations that Muslims in New Jersey celebrated the fall of the World Trade Center on 9/11, even as they criticized their veracity (Shafer, 2015).

Contrived controversies detract from coverage of important issues related to policy, process, and governance (Horton, 2017). In October of 2017, President Donald Trump and Senator Bob Corker (R-TN) exchanged a series of insults as Congress considered major tax reforms. The feud dominated coverage of the battle over tax legislation on new media, and commanded the front page of The New York Times. Among the many insults slung over the course of several weeks, Trump referred to Corker as "Liddle Bob," and tweeted that Corker "couldn't get elected dog catcher." Corker called the White House "an adult day care center," and labeled Trump "an utterly untruthful president" (Sullivan, 2017).

THE ASCENDANCE OF FAKE NEWS

The most extreme illustration of the concept of post-truth reporting is the rise of fake news. The definition of fake news has shifted over time, and continues to be fluid. Initially, the term "fake news" referred to news parodies and satire, such as The Daily Show, The Colbert Report, and Weekend Update on Saturday Night Live. During the 2016 campaign, the concept of fake news was attached to fictitious stories made to appear as if they were real news articles. These stories were disseminated on websites that had the appearance of legitimate news platforms or blogs, such as Infowars, The Rightest, and National Report. A 2017 compilation documented 122 sites that routinely publish fake news (Chao, et al., 2017). Authors are paid—sometimes thousands of dollars—to write or record false information. Some of these authors are based in locations outside of the United States, including Russia (Shane, 2017). They make use of social media interactions and algorithms to disseminate content to specific ideological constituencies. Fabricated stories are spread virally by social bots, automated software that replicates messages by masquerading as a person (Emerging Technology from the arXiv, 2017).

Fake news stories play to people's preexisting beliefs about political leaders, parties, organizations, and the mainstream news media. While some fake news stories are outright fabrications, others contain elements of truth that make them seem credible to audiences ensconced in echo chambers. Conspiracy theories, hoaxes, and lies were spread efficiently through Facebook, Snapchat, and other social media, and reached millions of voters in the 2016 election (Oremus, 2016). For example, a fabricated story on The Denver Gardian, a fake site meant to emulate the legitimate newspaper, The Denver Post, reported that an F.B.I. agent connected with an investigation into Democratic candidate Hillary Clinton's emails had murdered his wife and shot himself. Other erroneous reports claimed that Pope Francis had endorsed Donald Trump and that Hillary Clinton had sold weapons to ISIS (Rogers and Bromwich, 2016).

Conditions in the new media age have been ripe for the proliferation of fake news. The new media system has lifted many of the obstacles to producing and distributing news that were present in the previous mass media age. While vestiges of the digital divide persist, especially among lower-income families (Klein, 2017), barriers to new media access have been lowered. The cost of producing and distributing information on a wide scale have been reduced. The logistics and skills necessary to create content are less formidable. Social networking sites make it possible to build and maintain audiences of like-minded people who will trust posted content. Fake news proliferates widely through social media, especially Facebook and Twitter. In fact, fake news stories are spread more widely on Facebook than factual mainstream media reports (Silverman, 2016). Audiences are fooled and confused by fake news, which confounds basic facts about politics and government with fiction. A 2016 Pew Research Center report found that 64% of the American public found that made-up news created a great deal of confusion about the basic facts of current events, and an additional 24% believed fake news caused some confusion (Barthel, Mitchell, and Holcomb, 2016). Finally, legal challenges to fake news and the distribution of false content are much more difficult to pose, as it is costly and time-consuming to sue publishers for spreading false information.

An alternative meaning of fake news emerged after the presidential election. At his first press conference as President-elect, Donald Trump appropriated the term "fake news" as a derogatory reference to the mainstream press. Pointing at CNN journalist Jim Acosta, who was attempting to ask a question, Trump exclaimed, "You are fake news!" Trump and his acolytes frequently employ the "fake news" moniker when attempting to delegitimize the legacy media, including The New York Times and The Washington Post, for reporting they consider to be unfavorable (Carson, 2017). Weary of Trump repeatedly invoking the "fake news" label, CNN launched a "Facts First" campaign in response to "consistent attacks from Washington and beyond." A thirty second video shows an image of an apple, with the voice over:

This is an apple. Some people might try to tell you this is a banana. They might scream banana, banana, banana, over and over and over again. They might put banana in all caps. You might even start to believe that this is a banana. But it's not. This is an apple.

Donald Trump's Twitter account not only communicates decisions and sets goals but also responds aggressively to accusations.

Facts are facts. They aren't colored by emotion or bias. They are indisputable. There is no alternative to a fact. Facts explain things. What they are, how they happened. Facts are not interpretations. Once facts are established, opinions can be formed. And while opinions matter, they don't change the facts.

WATCHDOG PRESS OR POLITICIANS' MOUTHPIECE

The notion of the press as a political watchdog casts the media as a guardian of the public interest. The watchdog press provides a check on government abuses by supplying citizens with information and forcing government transparency. Public support for the media's watchdog role is substantial, with a Pew Research Center study finding that 70% of Americans believe that press reporting can "prevent leaders from doing things that shouldn't be done" (Chinni and Bronston, 2017).

New media have enhanced the capacity of reporters to fulfill their watchdog role, even in an era of dwindling resources for investigative journalism. Information can be shared readily through formal media sources; as local news outlets can pass information about breaking events to national organizations. News also can be documented and shared by citizens through social networks. When a vicious category 5 hurricane devastated Puerto Rico and the American government's response was slow, journalists were able to surface the story as residents and first responders took to social media to provide first-hand accounts to national journalists who had difficulty reaching the island (Vernon, 2017).

However, there are aspects of the media's watchdog role that have become more difficult to fulfill. Countering outright lies by public officials has almost become an exercise in futility, even as fact-checking has become its own category of news. The Washington Post's "Fact Checker" identified almost 1,500 false claims made by President Trump in just over 250 days in office (www.washingtonpost.com/news/fact-checker). Sites focusing on setting the record straight, such as PolitiFact, Snopes, and FactCheck, can barely keep pace with the amount of material that requires checking Despite these efforts, false information on the air and online has multiplied.

There is evidence to suggest that the new media allow political leaders to do an end-run around the watchdog press. In some ways, the press has moved from being a watchdog to a mouthpiece for politicians. This tendency is exacerbated by the fact that there is a revolving door where working journalists move between positions in the media and government. Some scholars maintain that this revolving door compromises the objectivity of journalists who view a government job as the source of their next paycheck (Shepard, 1997).

The media act as a mouthpiece for political leaders by publicizing their words and actions even when their news value is questionable. President Donald Trump uses Twitter as a mechanism for getting messages directly to his followers while averting journalistic and political gatekeepers, including high ranking members of his personal staff. Many of his tweets are of questionable news value, except for the fact that they emanate from the president's personal social media account. Yet the press act as a mouthpiece by promoting his tweets. A silly or vicious tween can dominate several news cycles. In an interview with Fox Business Network's Maria Bartiomo, President Trump gave his reason for using

social media to communication with the public and the press that supports the notion of the mouthpiece media:

Successful news media such as The New York Times or The Washington Post are often accused of publishing fake news when that information is not of the interest of some elites.

When rumors and conspiracy theories are believed, they can have serious consequences. This point is illustrated by the "PizzaGate" conspiracy theory that spread on social media during the 2016 presidential election. Democratic presidential candidate Hillary Clinton and her campaign chairman, John Podesta, were accused of engaging in satanic rituals where they personally "chopped up and raped" children. Wikileaks released personal emails from Podesta's account indicating that he enjoyed eating at a pizza restaurant Washington, D.C. The Twitter hashtag #pizzagate began trending. Rumors alleging that the restaurant's owner was running a child sex ring began circulating. Believing the rumors to be true, a man drove from North Carolina to liberate the purported child sex slaves. He fired an assault rifle inside the pizza restaurant as staff and patrons fled. He is currently serving a four-year prison sentence (Aisch, et al., 2016; Fisher, et al., 2016).

Conclusion

New media have both expanded and undercut the traditional roles of the press in a democratic society. On the positive side, they have vastly increased the potential for political information to reach even the most disinterested citizens. They enable the creation of digital public squares where opinions can be openly shared. They have created new avenues for engagement that allow the public to connect in new ways with government, and to contribute to the flow of political information.

At the same time, the coalescence of the rise of new media and post-truth society has made for a precarious situation that subverts their beneficial aspects. Presently, it appears as if there are few effective checks on the rising tide of false information. Substituting scandal coverage for serious investigative journalism has weakened the press' watchdog role. The ambiguous position of the media as a mouthpiece for politicians renders journalists complicit in the proliferation of bad information and faulty facts. It is important to recognize that American journalism has never experienced a "golden age" where facts always prevailed and responsible reporting was absolute. However, the current era may mark a new low for the democratic imperative of a free press.

References

1. Aisch, Gregor, Jon Huang, and Cecilia Kang. 2016. "Dissecting the #PizzaGate Conspiracy Theories," The New York Times, December 10.

2. Allcott, Hunt, and Matthew Gentzkow. 2017. "Social Media and Fake News in the 2016 Election," Journal of Economic Perspectives, vol. 31, no. 2: 211-236.

3. Barthel, Michael, Amy Mitchell, and Jesse Holcomb. 2016. "Many Americans Believe Fake News Is Sowing Confusion." Research Report. Washington, D.C.: Pew Research Center.

4. Camosy, Charles. 2016. "Trump Won Because College-Educated Americans Are Out of Touch," The Washington Post, November 9

5. Carson, James. 2017. "What is Fake News? Its Origins and How It Grew in 2016," The Telegraph, March 10.

6. Chinni, Dante, and Sally Bronston. 2017. "Despite Attacks on the Press, Public Supports Watchdog Role," NBC News, July 9.

7. Craig, Tim, and Michael D. Shear. 2006. "Allen Quip Provokes Outrage, Apology," The Washington Post, August 15.

8. Davis, Richard, and Diana Owen. 1998. New Media and American Politics. New York: Oxford University Press.

9. Diamond, Edwin, Martha McKay, and Robert Silverman. 1993. "Pop Goes Politics: New Media, Interactive Formats, and the 1992 Presidential Campaign," American Behavioral Scientist, vol. 37, no. 2: 257-261.

10. Duggan, Maeve, and Aaron Smith. 2016. The Political Environment on Social Media. Research Report. Washington, D.C.: Pew Research Center.

11. Emerging Technology from the arXiv. 2017. "First Evidence That Social Bots Play a Major Role in Spreading Fake News," MIT Technology Review, August 7.

12. Fisher, Mark, John Woodrow Cox, and Peter Hermann. 2016. "Pizzagate: From Rumor, To Hashtag, To Gunfire in D.C.," Washington Post, December 6.

13. Gil de Zuniga, Homero, Nakwon Jung, and Sebastian Valenzuela. 2010. "Social Media Use for News and Individuals' Social Capital, Civic Engagement, and Political Participation," Journal of Computer-Mediated Communication, vol. 17: 319-336.

14. Glasser, Susan B. 2016. "Covering Politics in a "Post-Truth" America," Brookings Essay, December 2.

15. Gottfried, Jeffrey, and Elisa Shearer. 2016. News Use Across Social Media Platforms 2016. Research Report. Washington, D.C.: Pew Research Center.

16. Graham, David A. 2017. "'Alternative Facts': The Needless Lies of the Trump Administration," The Atlantic, January 22.

17. Hayes, Danny, and Jennifer L. Lawless. 2015. "As Local News Goes, So Goes Citizen Engagement: Media, Knowledge, and Participation in U.S. House Elections," The Journal of Politics, vol. 77, no. 2: 447-462.

18. Hindman, Matthew. 2008. The Myth of Digital Democracy. Princeton: Princeton University Press.

19. Horton, Alex. 2017. "The Crazy Summer of Trump Controversies That You've Already Forgotten," The Washington Post, August 19.

20. Jamieson, Kathleen Hall, and Joseph N. Cappella. 2010. Echo Chamber. New York: Oxford University Press.

21. Keyes, Ralph. 2004. The Post-Truth Era. New York: St. Martin's Press.

22. Kiley, Jocelyn. 2017. "In Polarized Era, Fewer Americans Hold a Mix of Conservative and Liberal Views." Research Report. Washington, D.C.: Pew Research Center.

23. Linder, Matt. 2016. "Block. Mute. Unfriend. Tensions Rise on Facebook After Election Results," Chicago Tribune, November 9

24. Jebril, Nael, Erik Albaek, and Claes H. deVreese. 2013. "Infotainment, Cynicism and Democracy: The Effects of Privatization vs. Personalization in the News," European Journal of Communication, vol. 28, no. 2: 105-121.

25. Klein, Paula. 2017. "The 2017 Digital Divide," MIT Initiative on the Digital Economy, September 1. McChesney, Robert. 2015. Rich Media, Poor Democracy, 2nd Edition. New

Psychology in Physiotherapy

✍ **Sapna Jha**

Undeniably, the psychological component in physiotherapy could play a tremendous part in the results of the physical recovery but it is a fact that the **role of psychology in physiotherapy** is sometimes neglected. Physiotherapy, in general, is a whole-patient remedy for physical therapy involving the identification and treatment of psychological factors while promoting better healing and rehabilitation. It is more than a manipulation of how your body movements and anatomy are being affected. Psychological interventions in physiotherapy help with the people's management of their diseases, maintaining treatment regimens and gradually enjoying better outcomes.

The **role of psychology in physiotherapy** is to discover that the mind and the body function as the same system and are just not two different components while talking about psychology in physiotherapy. Moreover, just like how mental illness could lead to physical health conditions, the other way also works, meaning that a patient's physical health is also affected by his/her mental status. Therapeutic care provided by physical therapists must be a psychologically-oriented one given the inseparable connection.

Psychology, although easily neglected, is an essential element of successful physiotherapy that can have positive outcomes in physical rehabilitation. As a profession, physiotherapy is not just relying on physical conditioning, and manipulation of the body's muscles, and joints; it is a holistic approach to patient care that includes understanding psychological challenges in helping patients heal and recover faster. Simply, the addition of psychology to physiotherapy treatment aims to reduce stress, increase adherence to the treatment plan as well as ultimately lead to better outcomes.

One fails to oversee the role of psychology in physiotherapy as the bond between the body and the mind is interconnected and one has a meaningful impact on the other. The situation for the individual what is his/her mental state can also affect his/her physical health in ways, and on the other hand, some physical conditions can even influence a person's mental well-being. This establishes the interdependent relationship between the mind and the body and a psychological aspect is added to physical therapy.

Comprehending the Mentality of Sick Individuals

A **key role of psychology in physiotherapy** is comprehending the patient's mental condition. Health psychologists use many methods to assess if a patient is ready for physical therapy. They take into account things like the patient's degree of motivation, their expectations for the therapy, and any worries they may have about getting well. This helps therapists develop a plan that works for each patient's needs.

1. Creating a Healing Partnership

The relationship between physiotherapist and patient is a contextual formation based on empathy, trust, and a common goal. An accord capable of fostering mutual trust and respect may be considered a solid basis for the patients to commit to the proposed treatment schemes. Psychology as a subject lies at the very core of physiotherapy and here the physiotherapists focus on factors like the ability to communicate with patients on their terms as well as to address their issues which all enhance patient-therapist alliance.

2. Achieving Reasonable Objectives

A psychological tactic used in physiotherapy to increase motivation and give patients a sense of accomplishment is goal planning. Therapists assist patients in tracking their progress and remaining involved in their therapy by helping them develop reasonable and attainable objectives. Additionally, it helps control patient expectations and provides a positive outlook on recovery.

3.   Controlling Anxiety and Pain

Another important role of psychology in physiotherapy is the management of pain and anxiety. Methods like these:

- Psychological techniques, such as cognitive behavioral therapy (CBT), help people comprehend the connection between their emotions, ideas, and bodily experiences—especially pain.
- Therapists who integrate psychology into physical therapy can assist patients in creating individualized pain management regimens that take into account both the psychological and physiological components of pain.
- To assist manage the body's reaction to pain, relaxation methods including progressive muscle relaxation, guided visualization]
- , and deep breathing exercises are frequently taught.
- In physiotherapy, psychology also includes teaching patients about pain science, which helps them understand their suffering and lessen their tendency to avoid it.
- By using behavioural approaches, exercise levels are progressively increased under supervision, breaking the cycle of inactivity and muscular deconditioning that can make pain worse.
- Together, physiotherapists and psychologists create attainable functional goals that boost patients' self-esteem and promote following pain treatment guidelines.
- The utilisation of therapeutic interventions that include mindfulness-based stress reduction (MBSR) is one of the ways to

diminish the anxious symptoms that are related to the suffering of chronic pain where an individual can learn to focus on the current present.

- Given that psychological therapies involve the emotional dyings of pain in the rehabilitation process, they may very well contribute to the improvement of other rehabilitation procedures.

- To enable patients to properly manage acute pain episodes without jeopardising their overall treatment plan, self-regulation skills are taught.

- A complete pain treatment plan within physiotherapy includes psychoeducation regarding the appropriate use of pain medication, the necessity of a healthy lifestyle, and the advantages of physical exercise.

Motivation and Compliance

Motivational interviewing techniques are used by psychology in physiotherapy to assist patients in adhering to their treatment programmes and exercise schedules. One important psychological factor in the efficacy of physiotherapy treatments is motivation. Patients must discover an internal drive to be compliant and effective over the long run; these tactics help them do just that.

- Psychology is essential in the rehabilitation process because it helps patients cope with physical restrictions, whether they are temporary or permanent. Therapists collaborate with patients to create coping mechanisms such as:

- Psychology supports the evaluation of a patient's mental and emotional condition, which might impact how they react to physical trauma and how they heal.

- Patients who get psychological assistance are better able to perceive their rehabilitation as a purposeful move towards wellness as opposed to a reaction to impairment.

- Using psychological concepts, therapists create customised rehabilitation plans that tackle the psychological as well as the physical effects of an accident or impairment.
- Psychological therapies within rehabilitation environments might mitigate patients' perceptions of seclusion by motivating them to interact with support networks and local resources.
- Developing self-efficacy is essential because patients who have faith in their capacity to bring about change are more likely to stick with rehabilitation exercises and activities, which improves results.

Conclusion

The purpose of this review is to explore the historical development of physiotherapy as a profession in the context of present standards requiring physiotherapists to manage psychological issues that impact rehabilitation. The review will focus specifically on how the role of psychology in practice has evolved and whether this is reflected in current physiotherapy training programmes. Electronic papers were identified through a rigorous search of CINAL, AMED, MEDLINE, PsychINFO and EMBASE. Due to the historical exploration of this review, no time limits were applied to the searches and articles were retrieved as far back as 1894. The history of the profession demonstrates a very 'hands on' approach to treatment with minimal psychology related practices. Whilst numerous studies exploring psychology training in physiotherapy have reported significant inconsistencies across UK undergraduate physiotherapy programmes. Due to shifts in the dynamics of healthcare, it is apparent that physiotherapy programmes would benefit from including psychology skills training, as a core module, to meet these ever changing demands. Future research should explore what psychological interventions physiotherapists currently utilise in daily practice, as well as practitioner feelings on the standard and relevance of the psychology content provided in their formal training.

References

1. Arvaniti A, Samakouri M, Kalamara E, et al.. Health service staff's attitudes towards patients with mental illness. Soc Psychiatry Psychiatr Epidemiol. 2009;44(8):658–65. http: //dx.doi.org/ 10.1007/s00127-008-0481-
3. Medline:19082905 [PubMed] [Google Scholar]

2. van der Kluit MJ, Goossens PJJ. Factors influencing attitudes of nurses in general health care toward patients with comorbid mental illness: an integrative literature review. Issues Ment Health Nurs. 2011;32(8):51927. http://dx.doi.org/10.3109/01612840.2011.5713 60. Medline:21767254 [PubMed] [Google Scholar]

3. Harrison A, Zohhadi S. Professional influences on the provision of mental health care for older people within a general hospital ward. J Psychiatr Ment Health Nurs. 2005;12(4):472–80. http://dx.doi.org/ 10.1111/j.1365-2850.2005.00868.x.Medline: 16011503 [PubMed] [Google Scholar]

4. Australian Physiotherapy Association. Australian Physiotherapy Association position statement: chronic disease and physiotherapy. Hawthorn (VIC): The Association; 2009. [Google Scholar]

5. Australian Physiotherapy Association. Australian Physiotherapy Association position statement: pain management. Hawthorn (VIC): The Association; 2012. [Google Scholar]

6. Australian Physiotherapy Association. Australian Physiotherapy Association position statement: primary health care and physiotherapy. Hawthorn (VIC): The Association; 2008. [Google Scholar]

7. Australian Institute of Health and Welfare. When musculoskeletal conditions and mental disorders occur together. Canberra (ACT): The Institute; 2010. [Google Scholar]

8. Gureje O, Von Korff M, Kola L, et al.. The relation between

multiple pains and mental disorders: results from the World Mental Health Surveys. Pain. 2008;135(1-2):82–91. http://dx.doi.org/10.1016/j.pain.2007.05.005. Medline:17570586 [PubMed] [Google Scholar]

9. Korszun A, Young EA, Engleberg NC, et al.. Use of actigraphy for monitoring sleep and activity levels in patients with fibromyalgia and depression. J Psychosom Res. 2002;52(6):439–43. http://dx.doi.org/10.1016/S0022-3999(01)00237-9. Medline:12069867 [PubMed] [Google Scholar]

10. Morgan VA, Waterreus A, Jablensky A, et al.. People living with psychotic illness in 2010: the second Australian national survey of psychosis. Aust N Z J Psychiatry. 2012;46(8):735–52. http://dx.doi.org/10.1177/0004867412449877. Medline:22696547 [PubMed] [Google Scholar]

11. Galletly CA, Foley DL, Waterreus A, et al.. Cardiometabolic risk factors in people with psychotic disorders: the Second Australian National Survey of Psychosis. Aust N Z J Psychiatry. 2012;46(8):753–61. http://dx.doi.org/10.1177/0004867412453089. Medline:22761397 [PubMed] [Google Scholar]

12. Richardson CR, Faulkner G, McDevitt J, et al.. Integrating physical activity into mental health services for persons with serious mental illness. Psychiatr Serv. 2005;56(3):324–31. http://dx.doi.org/10.1176/appi.ps.56.3.324. Medline:15746508 [PubMed] [Google Scholar]

13. McLeod JE, Clarke DM. A review of psychosocial aspects of motor neurone disease. J Neurol Sci. 2007;258(1–2):4–10. http://dx.doi.org/10.1016/j.jns.2007.03.001 [PubMed] [Google Scholar]

14. Chen K, Fan Y, Hu R, et al.. Impact of depression, fatigue and disability on quality of life in Chinese patients with multiple

sclerosis. Stress Health. 2013;29(2):108–
12. http://dx.doi.org/10.1002/smi.2432. Medline:22566371 [PubMed] [Google Scholar]

15. Kurt A, Nijboer F, Matuz T, et al.. Depression and anxiety in individuals with amyotrophic lateral sclerosis: epidemiology and management. CNS Drugs. 2007;21(4):279–
91. http://dx.doi.org/10.2165/00023210-200721040-00003. Medline:17381183 [PubMed] [Google Scholar]

Role of financial literacies on wealth management

✍ Harsha

In India, only 27% of the population is financially literate, meaning only one out of every five Indians is equipped to deal with one of the most crucial aspects of human well-being. At the core of financial literacy lies the understanding of financial concepts and the ability to apply them in real-life situations. Wealth management goes beyond simply earning money; it involves strategic planning, allocation, and preservation of one's financial resources. Financial literacy acts as the guiding light in this process, allowing individuals to make informed choices that align with their long-term financial goals. The intersection of financial literacy and wealth management represents a critical nexus that profoundly influences individuals' financial well-being.

Beyond the basics: Understanding the curriculum of financial literacy

Understanding fundamental financial concepts such as budgeting, debt management, investments, and risk assessment is crucial for empowering individuals to make informed decisions about their finances. This comprehension allows people to establish effective budget plans, manage debts wisely, make informed investment choices, and assess and mitigate risks. Additionally, interpreting financial information, including statements, reports, and market fluctuations, is essential for active engagement in wealth management discussions.

How financial literacy helps in wealth management

Be your own informed decision-maker:

Financial literacy empowers individuals to make informed decisions about their finances. When managing wealth, individuals with high financial literacy levels are more likely to assess and understand the risks and rewards associated with different investment options. While it is important to seek advice from trusted sources, it is equally essential to avoid blindly following market trends. They can make decisions based on their financial goals, leading to a more tailored wealth management strategy.

Empowering your finances with self-taught investment mastery:

One of the key components of wealth management is investment. Financially literate individuals are better positioned to comprehend the various investment vehicles available, such as stocks, bonds, mutual funds, and real estate. They can evaluate the potential returns and risks associated with each investment, aligning their portfolio with their financial goals. A well-informed investment strategy is crucial for building and preserving wealth over the long term.

Be your own risk manager:

Wealth management involves navigating various financial risks. Financially literate individuals are better equipped to assess and manage these risks effectively. By aligning their decisions with financial goals, risk tolerance, and time horizon, they can craft a personalised and effective wealth management strategy, taking into account both external advice and their own understanding. This risk-aware approach is essential for safeguarding wealth against market fluctuations and economic uncertainties.

The responsible debtor:

Debt can either be a tool for wealth creation or a burden that hinders financial progress. Financially informed individuals grasp the distinctions among debt types, prioritising repayment of high-interest debts and sidestepping unnecessary accumulations. They navigate credit responsibly, understanding its potential for strategic use.

Digital lending companies offer quick credit access. Financially informed individuals utilise these sources, strategically tapping into credit for emergencies while aligning with broader financial goals.

Conclusion

Wealth management extends beyond the accumulation phase to include planning for retirement. Financially literate individuals are more proactive in planning for their retirement years. They understand the importance of starting early, maximizing contributions to retirement accounts, and optimizing investment choices to ensure a comfortable retirement. Adequate retirement planning is essential for maintaining financial stability during one's later years.

Financial literacy is a cornerstone of effective wealth management. As individuals enhance their financial knowledge, they empower themselves to navigate the complexities of the financial landscape, ultimately achieving their long-term financial goals and securing their financial future. It is imperative for individuals to invest time and effort in improving their financial literacy to unlock the full potential of their wealth management.

Wealth Management have access to a variety of resources including experienced portfolio construction, professional investment research, formal reviews, and exclusive investment benefits including access to the lowest costing investment share class, account aggregation, tax loss harvesting, and much more. We treat our clients like family and our advisors put you first. We offer investment management services, financial planning, consulting, and even a subscription service for those looking for regular financial advice that maybe aren't ready to have their assets managed.

References

1. Ameriks,John,RobertVeres,andMarkJ.Warshawsky.2001."Making Retirement IncomeLast aLifetime."JournalofFinancialPlanning, vol. 14, no. 12 (December):60-76

2. Arnott,RobertD.,AndrewBerkin,andJiaYe.2000."HowWellHaveTa xableInvestorsBeenServedinthe1980sand1990s?"

3. Barber,BradM.,TerranceOdean,andLuZheng.2005."OutofSight,Ou tofMind:

4. 4.Agarwal, S., Amromin, G., Ben-David, I., Chomsisengphet, S., & Evanoff, D. D. (2015). Financial literacy and financial planning: Evidence from India. Journal of Housing Economics, 27, 4-21

5. Aggarwal, M., & Gupta, M. (2014). Awareness of financial literacy among college students. Journal of Management Sciences and Technology, 2(1), 1-13.

6. 6.Agarwalla, S. K., Barua, S., Jacob, J., & Varma, J. R. (2012). A survey of financial literacy among students, young employees and the retired in India. Retrieved February, 26, 2013

Psychological Behaviour and Teens

✍ Amit

The adolescent years – roughly ages 12 through 24 are a developmental period characterized by pretty dramatic changes in multiple domains. Hormones are raging, emotions are high, brains are as yet "under construction", and teens tend to disconnect from family to focus on peers. While all of this is normal, it doesn't make it easy - on the adolescent or the parent.

This article walks through all the major developmental changes of adolescence, impacts of adolescent development on teen behavior and mental health, as well as how to support your teen during this developmental period.

Major Developmental Changes During Adolescence

The best description I ever heard about the psychology of adolescence was this: It's like starting the engines without a driver. The "engines" in this case are all the big emotions of the teenage years and the (absent) "driver" is the cognitive/self-regulatory functions that haven't quite come online yet. Let's walk through the major emotional, cognitive, and behavioral changes of the adolescent period.

Emotional development

We're all pretty family with the hormone changes that are happening in adolescence. And while it is true that puberty and all the hormone fluctuations that come with puberty can contribute to more intense emotions, there's another big contributor: changes in brain chemistry.

The adolescent body is working to establish its adult levels of two key neurotransmitters involved in emotion regulation - serotonin (a brain chemical involved in stress and negative emotions) and dopamine (a brain chemical involved in positive emotions). While these neurotransmitters are in flux as the underlying systems develop, there are two predictable emotional impacts on most adolescents:

(1) increases in negative emotions and heightened stress sensitivity, and

(2) decreases in positive emotions and suppressed positive reactivity.

Combined, this makes the typical adolescent more likely to experience negative emotions such as depression, anxiety, and anger and also to have a harder time experiencing positive emotions such as joy, enthusiasm, and connection. It's no surprise that teens can seem swamped by negative moods and unable to enjoy the things they used to enjoy! Their brain chemistry is simply not cooperating.

Cognitive development

While emotions are supercharged during adolescence, unfortunately the brain regions involved in emotion regulation are like tiny little triple-A batteries struggling to keep their device functioning. While the parts of the brain involved in emotional reactivity (the limbic system) are at full throttle, the brain regions involved in emotion regulation, impulse control, and decision-making (the prefrontal cortex) are the last to develop during the adolescent period - and they are not fully online until the mid-20s.

This means that teens often struggle to deploy good self-control and decision-making, especially in times of high emotion. They can appear to be self-focused, unable to anticipate future consequences, and highly susceptible to peer pressure and actions with immediate positive effects. They'll choose the instant gratification over the long-term positive benefit - the video game or snapchat conversation over studying or the drink at the party over the safety of getting home.

What's complicated for parents is that adolescent self-regulation can seem highly variable during this time - the same kid who can create a color-coded study guide for a final or explain the steps of a complicated video game to a sibling will make seemingly thoughtless decisions to forget to turn homework in, skip class, drink alcohol, or engage in a risky, thrill-seeking behavior. This is because the brain is developing during adolescence, it just isn't fully developed.

In conditions of low emotions, adolescents often appear as cognitively mature as adults. But in conditions of high emotion - including during peer interactions, when stressed, or when trying to impress other kids - they can struggle to effectively deploy good self-control or decision-making.

Behavioral development

The major psychological developmental tasks of adolescence are identity development and building autonomy. During this stage, teens need to learn who they are separate from their parents, siblings, and peers, and also start preparing to become less reliant on parents as they approach adulthood. While these goals are pretty clear, the paths towards them are often confusing and winding.

Impacts on Adolescent Behavior and Mental Health

The effects of the complex emotional, cognitive, and behavioral changes that come with adolescent development can be seen in changes in both behavior and mental health problems. Teens may seem more emotionally reactive, with more obvious anxiety, low mood, and irritability or angst. They may seem more sensitive to stress and over-reactive to previously minor situations. The combination of heightened emotions and underdeveloped cognitive regulation may manifest as poor impulse control, difficulties with decision making, sensation seeking, and risk taking behaviors.

For many teens, these emotional changes in combination with the increased stress of adolescence leads to an increase in mental health problems. The most common mental health concerns among teens are:

- **Anxiety** - Increases in worry, panic attacks, difficulty sleeping, and physical symptoms of anxiety (headaches, stomachaches) are some of most common symptoms of anxiety.

- **Social Anxiety** - Similar to anxiety, but the symptoms are typically in social or performance situations (social events, class presentations, tests, sports, or other peer to peer social interactions)

- **Depression** - Sad or irritable mood, not enjoying anything, low energy, low motivation, and difficulty sleeping are some of the most common symptoms of depression.

- **Self-injury** - Self-injury includes actions such as cutting, burning, picking, or head banging that causes some physical harm but is done without suicidal intent. A lot of research suggests that when stress or negative emotions are very intense, self-injury can relieve those emotions in the short-term - although it is a worrisome behavior in the long term. Increases in anxiety, depression, stress, and negative mood can be hard to tolerate.hen teens lack good coping skills, they will sometimes turn to self-injury to cope. This can be a sign teens need more support.

- **Substance use or other risky behaviors** - Some experimentation is relatively normal in adolescence, but many teens develop unhealthy habits with alcohol, marijuana, or other substances. This can result from sensation seeking (liking how the substances make them feel) and/or attempts to cope with negative emotions (liking the escape provided by substances). Unsafe use of substances in adolescence can have long term consequences and is also a sign teens need more support.

How to Support Your Teen

The tremendous amount of change happening in adolescence makes it a developmental period in which there is also a lot of potential for parents to have positive impacts on their teens' development. Learning how to express and regulate emotions, how to control behavior, how to make good decisions, and how to balance peer and family priorities are all important life skills that parents can shape through effective support. Some tips for coping with the complex psychology of adolescence:

1. **Model the behavior you want to see** - If you want your adolescent to learn how to express and regulate emotions in healthy ways, start by doing so yourself. Watch how you express emotions such as anger, disappointment, and anxiety. It is healthy to show these emotions, as well as show how you use adaptive coping skills to regulate them.

2. **Support independence and good decision making** - Like any life skill, teens have to practice how to make independent decisions to become good at it. As your teen gets older, give them more opportunities to do things independently, solve their own problems, and make decisions.

3. **Open communication** - Since many teens will naturally gravitate toward wanting more privacy and spending more time with friends, it is more important than ever to foster open and safe communication at home. Take time to check in with your teen daily, by taking a curious and nonjudgmental stance about their life. Ask more than you tell, and validate more than you correct. Being willing to touch the tough topics - sex, substances, and relationships - will make it easier for your teen to open up to you during this sensitive time.

4. **Know when to get them more help** - While some amount of increased moodiness and irritability is to be expected, along with variable motivation and focus in school, trust your gut when it comes to your teen's mental health. How might you know when

normal adolescent mood and behavior tips into worrisome territory? Look for persistence and impact. Down, anxious, or irritable mood that is consistent and lasts more than a week, and/or starts to affect grades, relationships, or safety are signs that your teen might benefit from therapy or more support.

Conclusion

Suicide-related behavior is complicated and rarely the result of a single source of trauma or stress. Youth who are at increased risk for suicide-related behavior are dealing with a complex interaction of multiple relationships (peer, family, or romantic), mental health, and school stressors. Often, people who engage in suicide-related behavior experience overwhelming feelings of helplessness and hopelessness. Involvement with bullying behavior is one stressor that may significantly contribute to feelings of helplessness and hopelessness that raise the risk of suicide. Youth are at higher risk for suicide-related behaviors if they experienced violence, including child abuse, bullying, or sexual violence, and cannot cope with problems in healthy ways and solve problems peacefully. Teens with disabilities, learning differences, sexual/gender identity differences, or cultural differences are often most vulnerable to being bullied. Teens who report frequently bullying others are at high, long-term risk for suicide-related behavior. Youth who report both being bullied and bullying others (sometimes referred to as bully-victims) have the highest rates of negative mental health outcomes, including depression, anxiety, and thinking about suicide.

References

1. Gallimberti, L., Buja, A., Chindamo, S., Lion, C., Terraneo, A., Marini, E., Gomez-Perez, L.J., & Baldo, V. (2015). Prevalence of substance use and abuse in late childhood and early adolescence: What are the implications? Preventive Medicine Reports, 2, 862-

867. https://doi.org/10.1016/j.pmedr.2015.09.018.

2. Kapetanovic, S., Boele, S., & Skoog, T. (2019). Parent-adolescent communication and adolescent delinquency: Unraveling within-family processes from between-family differences. Journal of Youth and Adolescence, 48(9), 1707-1723. https://doi.org/10.1007/s10964-019-01043-w.

3. Romm, K.F., Metzger, A., & Alvis, L.M. (2020). Parental psychological control and adolescent problematic outcomes: A multidimensional approach. Journal of Child and Family Studies, 29, 195-207. https://doi.org/10.1007/s10826-019-01545-y.

4. Salari, R., Ralph, A., & Sanders, M.R. (2014). An efficacy trial: Positive parenting program for parents of teenagers. Behaviour Change, 31(1), 34-52. https://doi.org/10.1017/bec.2013.31.

5. Siegel, D.J. (2013). Brainstorm: The power and purpose of the teenage brain. Jeremy P. Tarcher & Penguin.

6. Turner, R., Daneback, K., & Skarner, A. (2020). Explaining trajectories of adolescent drunkenness, drug use, and criminality: A latent transition analysis with socio-ecological covariates. Addictive Behaviors, 102, Article 106145. https://doi.org/10.1016/j.addbeh.2019.106145.

7. Van Noordt, S., & Willoughby, T. (2021). Cortical maturation from childhood to adolescence is reflected in resting state EEG signal complexity. Developmental Cognitive Neuroscience, 48, Article 100945. https://doi.org/10.1016/j.dcn.2021.100945.

8. Withers, M., McWey, L., & Lucier-Greer, M. (2016). Parent-adolescent relationship factors and adolescent outcomes among high-risk families. Family Relations, 65(5), 661-672. https://doi.org/10.1111/fare.12020.

Origin and evolution of economics and economic thought

The study of economic thoughts and the unity of their thoughts connects us with ancient times & help us to understand the origin of economic.

A study of Economic Thought provides a broad basis for comparison of different ideas. With the help of the study of economic thought student will realise that economics is different from economists.

The history of economic thought is the study of the philosophies of the different thinkers and theories in the subjects that later became political economy and economics, from the ancient world to the present day the 21st century.

According to professor Schumpeter 'Economic Thought' is the sum total of all the opinions and desires concerning economic subjects especially concerning with public policies of different times and places.

The origin of Indian economic thought provides the first overview of economic thought in the sub-continent the source of information available of the study of ancient economic thought are Vedas, the Upanishads, the Epics – Ramayana and Mahabharta, Manusmriti, Niti Shastras. Among these, the two most well known ancient Indian writings are 'Arthasastra' and Manusmriti. Kautilya was the important thinker, whose 'Arthasastra' has been considered the most reliable work on ancient economic thought.

Learning Objectives

This lesson is intended to tell you about the contribution some leading thinkers of Indian origin as well from the rest of the world relating to ideas in the field of economics.

- Some selected economic thinkers from India include: Thiruvalluvar, Kautilya, Dadabhai Naroji, Mahadev Govind Ranode, Ramesh Chandra Dutt, Gopal Krishna Gokhale, Mahatma Gandhi, Radha Kamal Mukherjee and Amartya Sen.

- The selected Economic thinkers from the rest of the rest of the world include: Adam Smith, David Hume, Luduring Von Mises, Thomas Malthus, J. M Keynes, Miton Friedman,

ECONOMIC THOUGHTS

Economic Thoughts of Thiruvalluvar (31 BCE)

Thiruvalluvar was a great Tamil poet and philosopher of ancient India. His famous work on ethics, namely, "Thirukkural" deals with the fundamentals of lifeand emphasised on righteous living in public life.Thiruvalluvar upheld adherence to spiritual and moral values for development of society. According to him, the four principles for a prosperous society are: (i) Faith in God (ii) Economic resources (iii) Spiritual leadership and (iv) Observance of moral law. The economic ideas of Thiruvalluvar are found in the second part of the 'Kural' which is named as Porutpal (dealing with wealth).

Some of the ideas of Thiruvalluvar can be stated as follows:

- Wealth is only means and not an end. Hording of wealth is bad and the hoarder is a burden to the earth.
- Society should be freefrom hunger, diseases and fear of external and internal aggression.
- Poverty and begging are the greatest social curses. Both should be eradicated.
- agriculture is very important for country as it is the source of food. There should be peasant proprietorship and no absentee landlordism.
- State has four functions: (i) creation of revenues, (ii) collection of revenues, 9iii) management of revenues and (iv) public expenditure. State must follow a systemof balanced budgeting and there should not be any compulsion in taxation.
- The King should promote education and health for all.

3.2.2 Economic Thoughts of Kautilya (375–283 BCE)

Kautilya is also known as Chanakya and Vishnu Gupta. He was a vedic scholar at the University at Taxila and latter became Prime Minister to Chandragupta who was founder of the famous Mauyra Empire which ruled over the mighty Indian empire in the 4th century BC. Kautilya is the author of "Arthasastra", one of the most important intellectual works in Indian history that covers almost every aspect of the theory of economics. It deals with material wealth, National Economy (Varta), agriculture & its allied activities, trade, dignity of labour, public finance, population, slavery, welfare state, social security, interest, price control, socio-economic institutions and town planning. The economic thoughts of Kautilya as given in "Arthasastra" are given in brief below:

➢ Wealth should be acquired through proper means and must be accumulated to protect people from famines.

➢ The King must learn about the science of national economy which was knownas Varta in order to discharge various functions successfully. Agriculture and animal husbandry, trade were included in Varta.

➢ National economy is most dependent on agriculture which happens to be the prime occupation of the people of the state. Hence the state and community were responsible for converting waste land for development of agriculture. The price of agricultural land would be based on its fertility. The state must intervene to fix the fair price of agricultural produce to discourage middlemen or traders to take advantage of the situation.

➢ Taxation was regarded as one of the most important sources of state revenue. But Taxes should not beburden and should be levied according to the ability to pay. Land revenue was the major source of tax for the state. Tax on commodities which entered into trade was also allowed.

➢ Kautilya was not in favour of slavery as was seen in other parts of the world at that time. He recognised the dignity of labour and recommended that hired labour be paid due wage as per contract failing which the employer would be subjected to pay fine to the King besides the due wages to labour. However, in case the labour was found to be a defaulter, then as per code of discipline the labourer must return back the wages taken by him.

 ➤ Regarding role of the state, Kautilya argued that the role of the state was to promote welfare of its people. The state must undertake those industrial activities which were important to promote self-sufficiency and self-reliance at national level. The state must also provide subsidies for development agriculture and allied activities and trade. Further state should regulate wage and working environment of workers, oversee production and distribution activitiesso that they were carried out efficiently. Private economic activities were also allowed under the state supervision.

Economic Thoughts of Dadabhai Naroji (1825-1917)

Dadabhai Naroji was a great educator, politician, social leader and an intellectual personality. He was the first Asian to become a British Member of Parliament (MP) in the House of Commons between 1892 and 1895. He was the first Indian to estimate the National Income of India. Naroji published a book,namely, "Poverty and un-British rule in India" in 1901. His book brought attention to the draining of India's wealth into Britain.

Dadabhai Naroji considered poverty as the major problem of India during the British rule. According to him, the continuous exploitation of India by the British Government and the consequent draining of Indian wealth to Britain was the reason for the poverty of the Indians. He estimated the per capita income in Bombay Presidency for the period 1867-70 Which was found to be Rs. 20. He concluded that this estimated amount was too low and far below the amount of Rs. 34 which was actually needed to meet the basic requirements during the same period. This finding of Naroji reflected poverty of the people of India. He further showed that Regressive Taxation System under the British rule was a major factor inpoverty.

Dadabhai Naroji propounded the theory of 'Drain of Wealth' in which he explained that from so many ways Britishers exploited Indian people and drain Indian wealth for their own country's Industrial progress. Narogi collected statistical data with respect to export, import, salaries of British Staff, railway construction etc and identified the factors responsible for drain of wealth. These factors are: (i) Large Remittances in the form of salaries and pensions for the British employees, (ii) Large Remittances from the savings and business profits to abroad by the Britishers, (iii) Payment for government expenditure in Britain and India.According to Naroji,the drain of wealth during colonial rule affected Indian capital formation badly. Free Trade policy adopted by the Britishers was actually a way to exploit India by offering highly paid jobs to foreign personnel. The East India ompany was purchasing Indian goods with money drained from India in order to export them to Britain.

Naroji believed that to solve the problem of the drain of wealth it was important to allow India to develop industries. He said that certain measures are needed to reduce Indian poverty some of which are given below:

1. Indian and Britain should pay all salaries to their people with their boundaries.

2. As the Britishers were paid reasonable or enough salaries while they served India, there was no need to pay pension to them.

3. As there was no danger of invasion of India by sea, India should not pay money for maintenance of navy.

Economic thoughts of Mahadev Govind Ranade(1842-1901)

Mahadev Govind Ranade was famous Lawyer and Economist. He was a subordinate judge in Pune in 1871. Given his political activities, the British government delayed his promotion to become a judge in Bombay High Court until 1895.His Economic thoughts are contained in different books and articles. His famous book - "Essays on Indian Political

Economy" published in 1898 provides lots of matter relating to his economic ideas and thoughts.

Ranade was very mush concerned about poverty in India. He outlined four major factors responsible for poverty in India: (i) Excessive dependence on agriculture, (ii) Defective land policy of the British government, (iii) Highly unorganized credit system and (iv) Backwardness of Indian Industries.

The remedies suggested by Ranade for removal of poverty and overall development of India can be summarized as follows:

India must follow the pattern of a planned economy and adopt the policy of welfare state. Ranade was against free trade and laissez-fare policy and market economy. Rather, he advocated the policy of protectionism for Indian industries since they were not capable of competing in the world market. There should be a balanced growth approach for the development of agriculture, industry and commerce in the country. There should be changes in the land policy which must include settlement of land tenure and ownership system for the benefit of farmers.

Economic Thoughts of Ramesh Chandra Dutt (1848-1909)

Ramesh Chandra Dutt was undoubtedly one of the great figures of his generation in India. He was one of the first Indians to get into the Indian Civil Service. Ramesh Chandra Dutt's pioneering work "Economic History of India" has earned him a permanent place in the history of Indian economic thought.

1. Dutt's Economic Thought on poverty gave a vivid description of the poverty of agricultural labourers in India. The condition of the people of India was described as miserable, critical, deplorable, pitiable and "no better than that of animals". He had also pleaded for reduction in the burden of land tax, reduce indebtedness of farmers, investments in rural roads, education, health, agricultural research, result in higher productivity growth, have a larger impact

on poverty reduction than do subsidies like fertilizer subsidies.

2. According to Ramesh Chandra Dutt povertyhas transformed scarcity into famines.

3. Dutt accepted the drain theory which explained that how developed countries drain the wealth of developing countries for their own benefits. He believed that all economic evils were the direct or indirect consequences of the imperialist economic policy of the British in India.

4. Ramesh Chandra Dutt dealt with the subject of public finance. As a true economist he had calculated the burden of taxation on Indian people. He contended that the incidence of taxation was about 8% in England and about 16% in India.

Economics thoughts of Gopal Krishna Gokhale(1866-1915)

Gopal Krishna Gokhale was the pupil of Shri Mahadev Govind Ranade. He was known as the political Guru of "Father of Nation Mahatma Gandhi". He expressed important views on economic, social and political matters. He was a great Philosopher, Social Reformer and a Economist. Gokhale's economic thoughts can be given briefly below:

1. Gopal Krishna Gokhale was against on those policies which supported Britishers and unfavorable to Indian economy. For example, the British government imposed heavy tax on salt and put the burden of loss on Indian people. Gokhale suggested that British government should reduce that salt tax.

2. Gokhle suggested Rent Regulation. He said that government should not take more than 20% of the total production.

3. Gokhale suggested that lack of Industrial development is the main cause of underdevelopment of the country. Lack of Industrial development is also the main cause of unemployment in less developed countries. So industrial development should be encouraged for the development of the country.

4. Gokhale recommended that functioning of financial system of government should be Autonomous. The government should curtail unnecessary defence expenditure and should not spend public income outside the country.

5. He gave more emphasized on equitable distribution on Income for the development of the country.

6. Gokhale suggested that in India Agriculture is the main source of employment. He was for all round development of agricultural sector.

Economic Thoughts of Mahatma Gandhi (1869-1947)

The economic thoughts of "Father of Nation Mahatma Gandhi" is based on truth and non-violence or spiritual thoughts. Gandhian Economic Thoughts are based on four fundamental principles–Truth, Non-violence, Dignity of labour and simplicity. Gandhi believed in simple living and high thining. Ghandhi opposed capitalism as it is based on the exploitation of human labour. According to Gandhi, Moral Progress is more important than material progress.

Gandhiji's Economic Ideas are the mixture of Ethicism, Socialism & Individualism. He believed that economics is a science of welfare state or welfare economy as same as western thinkers like Pigou, Marshall & Robbines etc. The method of study which was adopted by Gandhiji's was unique and based on ethical or moral values rather than inductive and deductive approach.

➤ Gandhi believed in the dignity of labour. God created man to eat his bread by the sweat of his brow.

➤ Gandhi opposed machines or use of machinery because if more machines or labour saving machinery will be used in production of goods and services then technological unemployment will exist in the economy.

➤ Gandhi was a sharp critic of large scale Industrialization, on the grounds of social justice. He believed that large scale industries or machines based industries destroy the handicrafts in villages. Machinery would enrich the few at the expenses of many. He advocated state ownership of public utilities.

➤ Gandhi advocated a decentralised economy. His decentralised include production at a larger number of places on a small scale. Thus, Gandhi wanted production by masses and not mass production. He wanted the revival of cottage industries.

➤ Gandhi has developed the principle of 'Trusteeship' which means that rich man should consider him as a trustee the society for all the wealth he accumulated.

Economic Thoughts of Radha Kamal Mukherjee (1889-1968)

Radha Kamal Mukherjee was born to a middle class family in Bengal and become involved in a growing mass movement for education and literacy while he was a child. Mukherjee studied about sociology & economics and he was interested in the economic structures of Indian villages, including commonly owned and managed resources such as irrigation channels and pastures, as well as mutual aid system for organizing work on large projects. He underlined two basic points—

1. Values are not limited only to religion or ethics.
2. Economics, Politics and Law also give rise to values.

Values are socially approved desires and goals that are internalized through the process of conditioning, learning or socialization and that become subjective preferences, standards and aspirations.

Economic Ideas of Mukherjee can be given briefly below:

1. Balanced Development Industries is essential for the growth of the nation.
2. Regional Economics in which regions are determined by regional Geography, Physiography, internal organic factors and historical traditions.

3. Institutional theory of economics can be studied both inductive and deductive methods.

4. Rural Reconstruction and Rural Planning – He believed that planned industrialization was essential to rural development.

5. He felt that economic planning had a great significance because of the growth of economic nationalism.

6. In his book 'the economic history of India', he described the changes that had taken place in agriculture, industry, trade, commerce, population etc.

Economics thoughts of Amartya Sen (1933-)

Amartya Kumar Sen born on 3rd Nov. 1933 is an Indian economist and Philosopher. Sen has made contributions to welfare economics, social choice theory, economics, and social justice, economic theories of famines, Decision theory, development economics, public health and measures of well being of countries. He awarded Nobel memorial Prize in Economic Science in 1998.

Amartya Sen's revolutionary contribution to development economics and social indicators is the concept of capability developed in his article equality of what. he argues that govt. should be measured against the concrete capabilities of their citizens.

1. He examined various meaning of poverty and drew attention to the incidence of absolute and relative deprivation. Head count ratio is the measure of poverty & inequality.

2. Sen produced a neat formula, termed as the poverty measure, known as the Sen index

2. P [1(1-1)G] H

3. Here P is poverty Index, 1 is the measure of distribution G is Gini coefficient, H is Head count Ratio.

4. The concept of capabilities developed by Sen as a better index of well being rather than commodities or utilities.

5. Entitlement – This concept refers to legally enforceable rights against the state like old age pensions in USA Sen has included in the concept of entitlement some more items like nutritious food, medical and health care, employments, security of food supply in times of famine etc.

6. Choice of Technique – Sen pleaded for adoption of capital intensive technique in a developing country like India because it will help in further expansion of the economy.

7. The Time series criterion – Sen argues that after getting the two time series of income & lows we have to apply the relevant rates of time discount.

8. Other Economic ideas –Sen was a favour of land reforms.

Conclusion

Truly speaking, Sen's contribution to applied economics is a momentous and relevant to the contemporary world as 'J.M.Keynes' theory of employment during the period of Great Depression about 7 decades ago.

Economics thoughts of David Hume (1711-1776)

David Hume was a great philosopher & Historical person. He was a contemporary of Adam Smityh. Davidhume's views on economics are express in his Essays, Moral, political and Literary, Part-II (1752).

David Lume (1711-1776) was a prominent intellectual of the Enlightenment. His books and essays generated radically innovative theories of human understanding, knowledge, religious belief, moral practice, aesthetic Judgement and political theory. Hume was not a pure advocate of laissez faire. He supported the infant industry argument. According to him the workers are employed either in agriculture or manufacturing. In the primitive societies, almost everyone is employed in Agriculture husbandry, and as agriculture techniques are improved, the land becomes able to support more non-agricultural workers, including artisans and providers of luxuries as well as manufacturers.

Economic thoughts of Adam Smith (1723-1790)

Adam Smith is known as founder of classical political economy and father of economics. He wrote his book "An Essay into the nature & "Wealth of Nation" in 1776 Economics can be defined as wealth of Nation. It means economics is a science in which we study about money, how we can earn money, how we can generate money and how we spend money. In other words according to adam smith economics mainly concern with money.

Economic Ideas of Adam Smith

1. Importance of Division of Labour – Adam Smith gave more importance to Division of labour. He started his book with these words. "The annual labour of every nation is the fund which originally supplies it with all the necessaries and conveniences of life which it annually consumes and which consist always either in the immediate produce of that labour or in what is purchased with that produce from other nations.

Adam Smith said that labour is the most important factor because with labour land & capital are useless.

According to Smith, "The greatest improvement in the productive powers of labour and the greater part of the skill, dexterity and judgment with which it is anywhere directed or supplied seem to have been the effects of the division of labour".

Theories of Adam Smith based on Naturalism and optimism Adam Smith principles are based on naturalism and optimism i.e. (1) Division of Labour (2) Money (3) Demand for money & supply of money (4) capital (5) Population (6) Demand and supply of the market.

These principles of Adam Smith is very famous & their existence is universal with these thoughts Adam Smith contribution in Economics always remembered or always considered remarkable.

Adam Smith favoured Laissez faire policy for the country and according to him functions of the Govt. could be classified into three groups.

1. Defence from foreign countries
2. Administration of legislation
3. Functions of Public welfare

Adam Smith gave two main principles of Natural value based theories:

1. Labour theory of value
2. Cost of Production theory of value

Conclusion: Adam Smith's contribution in Economic.

theories and in Principles is really unforgettable. It is truly said that economics is a science of wealth because in today's world whole economic activities are related with money.

Economic Thoughts of Thomas Malthus (1766-1834)

Thomas Malthus was an 18th century British Philosopher and economist known for the "Malthusian Growth Model". He gave more contribution in demographic theory and this theory states that population increases geometrically like 2, 4, 8, 16, but food production increases arithmetically like 1, 2, 3, 4. So, food production will not be able to keep up with growth in the population, resulting in diseases, famines war and calamity. He believed that we should limit population growth otherwise there is not going to be enough food to supply our huge population.

According to Malthusian theory, if people will not control the population then nature can control it. If increase in population is beyond the carrying capacity of the earth then these factors like war, famine and disease can control the population.

The Mercantilists believed that high population growth is good for the country because it provide more people to fight in army, work in factories and provide cheap services.

Malthus was a political economist who was concerned about what he saw as, decline of living conditions in 19th century in England. Malthus believed that population will be double in 25 years. He was pessimist and he thought that population can increase freely without taking any contraceptives, after a certain limit or beyond the carrying capacity of the earth, nature will control population itself by war, famines and diseases.

Conclusion: Although Malthusian thoughts were criticised by Neo-Malthusian economist but he gave great contribution in the study of population growth & how it affects the economy. Malthus must be regarded as the founder of the science of demography.

Economic Thought of Ludwig Von Mises (1881-1973)

Ludwig Von Mises happened to be a member of the Austrian School of Economics. He received his Ph. D in Law and Economics in 1906. Between 1913 to 1934 Mises worked as an economist in the Vienna Chamber of Commerce. During the same period, he was working as an unpaid professor in the University of Vienna. Because of this position Mises acted as principal economic advisor to the Austrian Government. In 1940 Mises emigrated to New York City and worked as Professor at New York state University from 1945 till his retirement in 1969.

Mises's ideas were based on the fundamental principle that individual human beings act purposively to achieve desired goals. This implies that he was a strong advocate of the policy of laissez-faire and no government interference in economic activities. Mises's contention was that government intervention would adversely affect market outcomes. He further argued that government intervention would create a socialistic form of society. For him socialism would be disastrous for a modern economy because of the absence of private ownership of land and capital goods that would prevent any sort of rational pricing or estimate of costs. His economic analysis itself was "value-free".According to Von Mises, expansion of free markets, the division of labour, and private capital investment are best possible ways to economic prosperity and flourishing of humanity.

The Austrian School of Economics led by Mises believed that expansionary bank credit encouraged by Central Banks is primarily responsible for inflation and depression and hence remains as major factor that cause business cycle in the economy. This view was also supported by most younger economists in England as the best explanation of the great depression that shook the capitalist worldduring the early 1930s. Mises advocated for reduction in bank credit to control inflation and adoption of laissez-faire policy during recession.

In his famous and one of the best seller books of its time, namely, "The theory of money and credit" published in 1912, Mises applied the concept of marginal utility in explaining demand for money. He opined that money is demanded for its utility to buy other goods rather than for its own sake.

Economic Thoughts of J.M. Keynes (1883-1946)

J.M. Keynes (1883-1946) was an early 20th century British economist, best known as the founder of Keynesian economics and the father of Modern Macro Economics. He has given great contribution in World Wide Depression period (1929-33), when U.S.A & U.K. were suffering from the problem of unemployment due to depression. At that time Keynes wrote his book "The General theory of employment, interest & money" published in 1936. Keynes believed that Aggregate demand play very important role in economy. But classical thinkers gave more importance to Aggregate Supply. Classical economists like Adam Smith, Malthus, Ricardo & J.B. Say etc. were failed to solve the problem of depression because their thoughts was that supply remain always equals to Demand & no problem of under production & over production arise in the economy. But Keynesian believed was that economy is Dynamic & Aggregate Demand & Aggregate Supply may be equal or may not be. So when world was facing the problem of Depression & Producer's unsold stock was increased, at that time Keynes said that if Aggregate supply remains constant only Aggregate demand increases then all unsold stock will be demanded by consumers and in this way producers will encourage to produce in future and production will rise. Due to rise in production, employment will rise & problem of unemployment will solve.

Keynesian economic ideas were innovativeand provide better understanding of macroeconomics.

> Keynes advocate the role of government is necessary to curb unemployment and to establish economic stability in the economy.

> Keynes believed that saving & consumption both are the function of income. As well as income rises consumption & saving will rise.

> Keynes developed the concept of multiplier & he explained multiplier concept as an investment multiplier, which shows the ratio of change in income due to change in initial investment.

> According to Keynes, money is very liquid form of asset & people always demand for money for particularly three purposes which are: 1) Transaction Purpose 2) Precautionary Purpose 3) Speculative Purpose.

> Classical thinkers believed that investment depends upon rate of interest & it is inversely related to rate of interest. But according to Keynes investment depends upon the future expectations of the capital asset and desire of the investors not only to the rate of interest.

> According to Keynes, "Interest is the reward for parting with liquidity for a specified period. It is a reward for not hoarding."

Keynes's influence has been extraordinarily great in the field of economics.

Economic Thoughts of Milton Friedman (1912-2006)

Milton Friedman was an American economist best known for his advocacy of free-market capitalism. His major contribution has been in the field of monetary economics. He was graduated in economics from University of Chicago and got his Ph. D degree in economics from Columbia University in 1946.Friedman's contributions to the field of economics started in a serious note during his 30 years of active teaching and research activities at University of Chicago. He strongly believed that free market mechanism has the potential to solve economic problems facing the individuals and society. That is why he was known as a critique of Keynesian school of thought which prescribed government intervention to boost demand in the economy. If Keynes dominated the first half of the 20th Century through his ideas relating to fiscal policy and role of government, Milton Friedman exercised extraordinary influence in the latter half of 20th century by advocating the role of free market and use of monetary policy to achieve economic stability. In fact, the intellectual community led by scholars like Friedman at University of Chicago which believed in the principles of free-market capitalism and importance of monetary policy has been famously known as the "Chicago School of Economics".

Some significant contributions of Friedman can be stated as follows:

➢ In his famous theory of consumption function, Friedman argued that people's annual consumption is a function of "permanent income" and not "current income" as argued by Keyes earlier. Friedman's "Permanent Income Hypothesis" says that people smoothen their spending based on what they expect their income to be in the long term.

➢ In his book titled "Capitalism and Freedom" published in 1962, Friedman propagated the idea of free market among the common public. The book became the best-selling intellectual work of the 1960s in which Friedman argued for a negative income tax to remove poverty, free market for allocation of resources and determination of prices including exchange rates etc.

➢ Milton Friedman is popularly known for "Monetarism", a term used to describe the importance of monetary policy in bringing about economic stability. Friedman believed that Central Bank of the country is responsible for fluctuation in price level which is known as inflation or deflation. So, control of money supply holds the key to control inflation or deflation.

For his extraordinary work Friedman was awarded the Nobel Prize for economic science in 1976.

List of Contributors

S.No.	Authors' Description
1	Sahil Srivastava (Gold Medalist) BSc. (Nursing), C.C.S. University, MSc. (Nursing), A.B.V.M.U., MAPC (Psychology), IGNOU Nursing Tutor, Kailash Institute of Nurisng and Para-Medical Science, Greater Nioda sahil.srivastava@gmail.com
2	Shailendra Mishra B.A. (Hindi and Economics), Lucknow University and M.A. Economics, Awadh University. Senior Correspondent Bharty DD News, DD Bhawan, Copernicouse Marg, Mandi House, New Delhi-110001 Solve200@yahoo.co.in
3	Saket Kumar B.Com., Delhi University, L.L.B., C.C.S. University, MAJMC, IGNOU, M.A. (Political Science), VMOU, M.Com., IGNOU SHO, Barakhamba Road, New Delhi Sakdp7@gmail.com
4	Ashima Thakur B.Com., M.Com., MBA (Finance), UGC-NET *PhD. Research Scholar, Desh Bhagat University, Gobindgarh (Punjab) Ashima.thakur151@gmail.com
5	Siddharth Kumar Bansal BSc. Forensic Science, Amity University, MSc. Forensic Science, Chandigarh University, DMS (IIBMS)

	Professional Digital Forensic and Academic Researcher Bansalsid2@gmail.com
6	Dr. Tarun Chauhan M.Com., PGFAM (London, UK), DMS, M.Phil., PhD. IIP Post-Doctoral (USA) Academic Coordinator and Associate Faculty, IGNOU Regional Centre Guest Professor, Sri Guru Gobind Singh College of Commerce, Delhi University. New Delhi amr.academy@uninxt.com
7	Sudesh Kumar B.A, M.A., PGDT, BLIS, PGJM Judicial Translator Delhi High Court, New Delhi-110059 goodsudeshkuma@gmail.com
8	Manurut Tokas Ph.D. Research Scholar, G.D. Goenka University Manurut101@gmail.com
9	Puja Roshani M.Com., M.Phil., PhD. Assistant Professor, CMS Jain University, Bangalore pujasomde@gmail.com
10	Prarthna Singh BBA & MBA Symbosis International University HR Manager, Nitigya Buildcon, Pvt., Ltd., Gurugram Prarthna120@gmail.com
11	Harsha B.Com. Rajdhani College, Delhi University, MBA (Finance), IGNOU

	Freelancer harshabarkaodiy@gmail.com
12	Sapna Kumari BPT, MPT (sports), C.C.S. University Fitphysioga Clinic, Greater Noida Sapnna2@gmail.com
13	Amit BPT, C.C.S. University, MPT, IIMT University Tutor, Sharda University, Department of Physiotherapy, School of Applied Health Science, Greater Noida amit.54@sharda.ac.in
14	Reena Bajaj B.A., M.A. (Economics) Academic Counselor, IGNOU Reena.bajaj1367@gmail.com